MAKE IT IN SHOWBIZ
Life Behind the Scenes

J.D. SOUTHERS

Copyright © 2024 by B-Listed Media, Inc.

All rights are reserved, and no part of this publication may be reproduced, distributed, or transmitted in any manner, whether through photocopying, recording, or any other electronic or mechanical methods, without the explicit prior written permission of the publisher. This restriction applies to any form or means of reproduction or distribution.

Exceptions to this rule include brief quotations that may be incorporated into critical reviews, as well as certain other noncommercial uses that are allowed by copyright law. Any such usage must adhere to the specified conditions and permissions outlined by the copyright holder.

Published by B-Listed Media, Inc.

Book Design by HMDPUBLISHING

Acknowledgments

Thanks to my mom for instilling an unwavering faith in God and exposing me to the arts. Thanks to my dad for leading by example and raising me to value leadership, community, and family.

Thank you to my brothers. I got to watch your grit and entrepreneurial spirit first-hand. Also, to my nieces and nephews on their own journey in entertainment. To my aunt Lorraine for the valuable advice in my adulthood and cousin P, the north star, for following your dreams.

Thanks to those who have supported me professionally. Entertainment Attorney Anuj Gupta and FirstGen Law, who jumped in first to support me. Business coach Michelle Levister and Perceive LLC. Author and coach Rev. Melony McGant, for encouraging me to write. Fellow creative friends Claudia, Miguel, Stacy, and Kelli, for your help nurturing my creative aspirations—thank you!

Contents

Preface 5
01. A Brief History of the Film Industry 12
02. Identify Your Talent and Interests 33
03. Research Different Niches. 44
04. Create Your Unique Brand 57
05. Navigating the Competitive Landscape 66
06. Skills, Certifications, and Education 75
07. Land a Gig. Be a Rockstar on Set. 82
08. Get Your Work Noticed. 101
09. Union vs. Non-Union: To join or not to join?.......... 112
10. Sustain a Successful Career in the Industry 121

Conclusion 130
Glossary... 133
References 140

PREFACE

*"You are not defeated when you lose.
You're defeated when you quit."*
— **Paulo Coelho**

This book provides real-world practical advice. However, with all things, there are exceptions. I refer to those exceptions as my personal experiences or "POV." These chapters contain my POV of *life behind the scenes*.

This compilation of information comes from the last eight years I've spent journaling my experiences as I transitioned from working a menial 9 to 5 job I hated to that of a full-time freelancer in the entertainment industry. I don't proclaim to be a millionaire or a high-level executive. Still, I have been successful in my own right, and my opportunities continue to trend upward after eight years of dedicated focus. I put this blueprint together for the dreamers, young creative, and the late bloomers, like me, who have so much fire inside that, if pointed in the right direction, with the right tools and opportunities, can live a life of passion and purpose too and thrive at any stage.

If you think you want to enter showbiz to make a ton of money, I'll tell you right now that you're getting into it for the wrong reasons. If you go down this path, it should be connected to something deep within you that drives you forward. This will be where you pull your strength from when you must spend multiple back-to-back 12-hour days on a production set.

I also must warn you that this is a very lonely journey—especially if you are transitioning from one industry to this one. Your friends and family will think you've gone mad. Why would you give up stability to work on an entry-level production gig that barely lasts two weeks? They expect you to hit rock bottom, tuck your tail between your legs, lick your wounds, and head back to your safe 9 to 5. For me, that reason alone was enough motivation to keep going.

This was never a pursuit of wealth but one of passion. It kindled in my childhood and drove me to great lengths, even going so far as settling in an entirely new city. At the time, my hometown didn't have a movie scene. Fast-forward 10 years later, and that hometown now has a robust production scene. I had the pleasure of returning home to assist in casting two Netflix productions. Not having many friends and family who could understand this journey, I turned to someone I had admired from a very young age—the now an Oscar-nominated and Grammy Award-winning music and film producer.

I first met my cousin P in Virginia Beach at our annual family reunion in my pre-teen years. I vividly remember the convo we had when I was almost 13 years old. When he walked into the room, he had a presence about him that he would be somebody and would be going places. I asked him, "What do you do?" He confidently responded, "I'm a music producer in a group called The Neptunes."

He perhaps saw the confusion on my face, not understanding that this was an actual career path. He continued, "Do you know the song Rumpshaker?" I immediately perked up and said, "Yes, I love that song!" He smiled. This 13-year-old girl knew his work.

Then, a year later, I was sitting at home after school, watching a popular music show on the BET network called *Rap City*, which I watched daily. Imagine my shock as a teenager when a new music video premiered on TV, and featured in this music video, sitting and rapping the hook alongside the artist, was my cousin P, better known as Pharrell.

I couldn't believe it. He told me who he'd be, and he became just that and eventually much more. It almost seemed overnight. But success is never overnight. At that moment, I understood the power of manifestation and speaking things into existence.

I spent my earliest years in performing arts, attending a performance arts school for theatre in middle school and in high school musicals and one-act plays. The biggest and most important time of high school for me was the spring musical, being nominated for Best Musical, and performing at the Gene Kelly Awards. The Gene Kelly Awards are a bonified Tony Awards for high school students today. We were the high school musical before *High School Musical*.

That's Mr. B in the picture with the white mustache at rehearsal for our production of the musical *Once Upon a Mattress*. Originally starring the lovely Sarah Jessica Parker on Broadway. Mr. B was a force to be reckoned with. He was our theatre director and a surrogate father to many of us. After my father passed away in ninth grade, I was completely devastated. My #1 fan was gone. I withdrew from friends and retreated into myself. The only things that kept me going were the spring musicals and Mr. B. He looked so much like my dad with his stature, mannerisms, and stern features. See, this is my dad with the bow tie. Can you see the resemblance? Like my dad, Mr. B never once hesitated to yell at us if we were slacking off and pushed us to be greater. However, ev-

Preface

eryone adored Mr. Babusci. Also, like my dad, he instilled in us an unparalleled work ethic. As teenagers, we rehearsed until 11 pm on school nights and didn't think twice about it. Mr. B taught us about *magic* and how to create, harness, and leave it on the stage for others to witness.

I was exposed to the Arts my entire life, but I fell in love with TV and film when my god-sister Senita took me backstage at BET, where she worked as a producer. That was a point in time when BET was in its prime, and Big Lez, Da'Jour, Joe Clair, Ananda Lewis and others were household names.

By the time I got to college, I knew exactly what industry I was going into. So, I majored in media communications. My next-to-youngest brother, a DJ and party promoter, helped me land an internship at the radio station. I was 19 years old and promoting celebrity events at functions and nightclubs for the radio station. He was well-known around the city for his parties, so I helped collect his payment at the door on many occasions. Working in promotions was right up my alley. I had plenty of polaroids of the promo work I was engaged in at 19 with the biggest names in the industry. I was on my way. Or so I thought.

Still, I hadn't had any opportunities for film. The industry was non-existent in my small hometown at the time. All I could think was how in the world I would get out of this city and make it to Hollywood. At that time, the only place film production had a presence was Los Angeles. If you couldn't get there, then forget about it.

Looking back, I sometimes get emotional that I almost gave up and took a decade off from my dream because I didn't have a blueprint, a mentor or anyone who had gone down the path I did—except for P. However, after college, I wouldn't connect with him for another eight years until the rise of social media platforms, and by this time, he had already reached superstardom.

Usually, superstars become out of reach and even out of touch and for good reasons. However, we reconnected over the years, and in my journey, he always found a moment to pay it forward and share his wisdom from his experiences.

In my hiatus from my dream, my next-to-oldest brother, a protégé of the late playwright August Wilson, was also in the earlier stages of his artistic journey. A decade later, my brother was in a catastrophic accident that left him immobile for quite some time. I stepped in with no experience to manage his theater for a year. In that role, I got to wear many hats, oversaw marketing, fundraising, and strategic planning around the theater's grants, and managed production vendors. I also digitized their files, refreshed the brand and updated the website. I realized I was pretty good at working in multiple areas.

It wasn't until I created a Facebook ad campaign that went viral of a video I produced with footage I had captured on the opening night of the show at August Wilson's childhood home that I found a new talent. After discovering my knack for digital marketing, I applied to Barack Obama's *Organizing For Action*, which had been instrumental in his success through grassroots and small-dollar donations. It was the first of its kind in the developing digital landscape. I was selected as a digital content fellow to learn how to leverage digital skills in impactful ways, along with a free trip to its Chicago headquarters. This is how I learned to embrace new roles, build new skills, and discover hidden talents.

A couple of summers ago, the theater I once managed for my brother debuted its theater season at the star-studded grand opening of the newly renovated August Wilson House, an arts hub commemorating the late playwright. Denzel Washington and other big names from the entertainment industry (Oprah, Tyler Perry, film director Antoine Fuqua (also from my town), and many others) contributed through donations to this event with opening remarks from Pittsburgh's mayor. If you look closely, you can spot Mr. Washington on the far right and my brother directly to his left.

Preface

August Wilson's Broadway play *Fences* was turned into an Oscar-winning film directed and produced by Denzel Washington. My late grandmother's house pictured here was the video village and production office. My grandma's house even made a cameo in the trailer with kids playing baseball in the street. Hers is the house on the corner with the awning. The film scene in Pittsburgh had become robust after my departure. It was literally at my back door. Go figure!

My eldest brother and niece provided catering for the cast and crew and was Denzel Washington's trusted go-to for his meals anytime he came to town. Fast-forward to the present day, my niece has officially joined the IATSE union and is making a career for herself in the industry, working on a hit series right in our hometown. The apple doesn't fall too far from the tree in our family, as you can see. Heck, my next-to-youngest niece is 13 and dabbling in anime and animation with her dad. I imagine she'll be working at Pixar by the time she's my age.

My, how times had changed in a decade. Now, Hollywood was everywhere, in cities all across America. The opportunities opened up avenues I could only have dreamed of when I graduated college.

If you want to break into the industry, now is the time. Production is everywhere, and with this companion guide to help you navigate the terrain, you can learn from the experiences I've gathered in this book. I do this for the younger me who had the sparkle in her eyes—the same sparkle I see in everyone else who aspires to dream big and comes from small towns. This is my way to pay it forward.

I wrote this preface after I sat in the movie theater alone, watching the movie credits roll up on the big screen and holding my breath, hoping to see my name in the credits but scared that maybe they forgot to acknowledge my contributions to the film's casting. Being unacknowledged had become a theme throughout my life. I finally saw my name roll up the screen. I was completely overcome with joy. At that moment, I felt like maybe I had made up for the time I had lost after almost quitting.

One of my favorite books, *Outliers: The Story of Success,* by Malcolm Gladwell, examines what makes talented and exceptional people extremely successful at the outer edge of what is statistically plausible. He examines the likes of Bill Gates, Mozart, The Beatles, and other outliers and compares them to other lesser-known but equally talented individuals to draw comparisons. His thesis was that individual success is a myth. That a supportive community is crucial to success and that being an outsider can, at times, work in your favor by driving you to work harder through meaningful work—that provides autonomy, complexity, and reward based on effort, cultural legacy, and opportunity are the drivers to success. He believes that society has a duty to make success more available to those who want to put in the hard work to make a lasting impact on the world.

The most popular concept from the book that shifted my mindset about what I was willing to dedicate to my dreams was what he referred to as the "10,000-hour rule". In a nutshell, it states that it takes this amount of hours of concentrated deliberate practice to develop your full potential. With drive, a talent for your niche, deliberate practice, opportunity, and community (and this book), you'll be on your way.

As you can glean, I am grateful to be walking in my purpose, approaching my 10,000 hours and here to guide you toward yours.

CHAPTER ONE:
A BRIEF HISTORY OF THE FILM INDUSTRY

Over the years, the American film industry has undergone significant transformations and is now a thriving domain. From silent films to digital cinema, it has faced countless changes and challenges while seizing opportunities along its journey.

The history of American cinema dates to the late 19th century, with Thomas Edison's *The Great Train Robbery* being one of its first ventures into silent movies in 1903. Hollywood emerged as an entertainment capital during the Roaring Twenties, dominated by major studios like Paramount and MGM, leading up until sound-on-film was integrated and became revolutionary for filmmaking, giving birth to the talkies era.

Hollywood's Golden Age from the '30s-'40s produced classic movies such as *Gone With The Wind*, with iconic faces including Clark Gable and Marilyn Monroe taking center stage on-screen, marking monumental moments within the cinematic space.

Furthermore, following World War II, important developments resulted from the rise of television, which prompted innovation, culminating in technicolor widescreen formats that adopted new technologies. These developments made arthouse directors ascend their ranks, creating larger-scale blockbusters from the 1970s to the 1990s, introducing franchises such as *Indiana Jones* and *Jurassic Park* that became household names.

However, technological improvements and streaming services have changed distribution patterns. Among other things, these changes have not stifled growth; nonetheless, this does not diminish Hollywood's continued domination as an acting global superpower, shaping current, popular, and cultural phenomena.

In this chapter, we will assess recent trends, current issues, and future potential in the film industry through careful research.

OVERVIEW OF THE INDUSTRY

The film industry, a global juggernaut, generates billions of dollars in income each year. According to Statista, the global box office generated $42.5 billion in 2019. This is largely so because the industry is diverse, with areas such as film production, distribution, exhibition, and home entertainment.

Film production is the creative hub where movies, TV shows, and other visual content come to life, involving stakeholders such as studios, independent producers, and streaming platforms.

The distribution segment markets and transports these creations to theaters, streaming services, and other outlets for exhibition. Exhibition refers to the screening of motion pictures with a theatrical release.

TRENDS IN THE INDUSTRY

The film industry is continually changing because of technology breakthroughs, shifting consumer preferences, and developing trends.

The Rise of Streaming Platforms

Streaming services such as Netflix, Amazon Prime, Disney+, and Hulu have transformed the traditional film industry by allowing users to watch movies and TV shows from the comfort of their own homes or handheld devices. According to Statista, Netflix's global subscriber base alone hit 167 million in the first quarter of 2020. Streamers are reluctant to share their subscriber numbers as they compete for market share.

International Market Growth

The film business is becoming more global, with emerging economies such as China, India, Africa, and Latin America driving expansion. According to the Motion Picture Association (MPA), International box office income reached $31.1 billion in 2019, accounting for 73% of total global revenue.

Interestingly, According to consultancy firm Ormax Media, Bollywood's cumulative box office in 2023 pulled in $1.3 billion, making it one of the best-grossing years of all time. Bollywood's resurgence has been driven by diverse content offerings, innovative marketing, and pent-up demand among audiences for experiencing movies on the big screen, notwithstanding the rise of streaming platforms.

Also, there has been an influx of new content from Nollywood on Netflix. Movies like *Ijakumo: The Born Again Stripper (2023)*, *Jagun Jagun (2023)*, and *Chief Daddy (2022)* had massive viewership, including international viewership.

A Tribe Called Judah, directed by Funke Akindele, has made headlines in the Nollywood film industry by achieving the title of the highest-grossing film in 2023. With a remarkable box office earnings of 400 million naira within just 12 days, the movie has set a new standard. Notably, it secured the record for the biggest weekend opening in Nollywood, amassing over N122 million at the box office.

Furthermore, following its retention of the world's largest film market in both 2020 and 2021, China ceded its box office crown to North America in 2022. China's cinema ticket sales were just 30 billion yuan, a 36% decrease from the previous year and less than half of pre-pandemic levels. Pandemic restrictions, interruptions in movie development and distribution, and competition from video streaming services have significantly impacted the business.

Prior to the outbreak of the epidemic, China was neck and neck with Hollywood, earning over $9 billion at the box office with robust market demand. Nonetheless, recent consumer surveys have shown a clear preference shift from cinema experience to online video alternatives, which was expected to stay in the aftermath of the pandemic.

Emphasis on Diversity and Inclusion

Diversity and inclusion are becoming more important in the industry, with greater chances for women, people of color, and other historically underrepresented groups. This trend is driven by shifting consumer tastes and social movements such as #MeToo, #BLM, and #OscarsSoWhite. This even led to NBC announcing in 2021 that its annual televised Golden Globes ceremony would not be aired. The Hollywood Foreign Press and a prestigious ceremony akin to the Academy Awards host the Golden Globes. At that time, it was rejected by A-list celebrities like Tom Cruise, Scarlett Johansson, and Mark Ruffalo.

Technological Breakthroughs

In the film industry, technological breakthroughs such as virtual reality, augmented reality, 3D cinema, and artificial intelligence (AI) have considerably improved the movie-going experience. AI, however, has been more controversial than its predecessors. We'll look at it a bit closer in the upcoming sections of this book.

CHALLENGES FACING THE FILM INDUSTRY

The film industry also faces various challenges that impact its growth and profitability. Some of the key challenges facing the industry include the following:

Piracy

Illegal downloads and streaming of movies and TV shows constitute a substantial challenge for the industry, resulting in losses of billions annually. Also, streamers like Netflix have been adamant about cracking down on password sharing to increase their subscription base. Contrary to public outcry, Netflix has not abandoned those efforts to crack down on password sharing.

Competition

The film industry battles intense competition from other entertainment forms, including video games, social media, and sports. We are witnessing the emergence of gamified movie and TV experiences that allow you to pick your own endings. Netflix has a dedicated department that focuses on including gaming on its streaming platform.

Rising Costs

The cost of producing and marketing big-budget films and TV series has put increasing pressure on studios to focus on profitability over taking bold risks at the box office, renewing a series, or greenlighting a new project that may have a niche audience regardless of how well done it is because of costly productions that eat away at the bottom line. With such a focus on profitability post-pandemic, production studios may be more inclined to take less risk when it comes to new and diverse filmmakers that can address its ongoing diversity dilemma. The upside for streamers and fans of subscription services is that they don't have to rely solely on original content and can license fresh and new content from independent studios and filmmakers worldwide. The downside for streamers is that our extreme content-binging makes it challenging for streamers to constantly have a catalog that is attractive enough for subscribers not to cancel one subscription and hop over to another streaming service. You'll notice streamers returning to the days of old and releasing weekly episodes to slow down our need to binge content at a rapid pace.

COVID-19 Pandemic

The COVID-19 pandemic has significantly impacted the film industry, with cinema closures, production shutdowns, and delays in release dates.

During the pandemic, as movie theaters were shuttered, A-list actors found opportunities elsewhere by starring on popular streaming platforms. Even film distributors partnered with streaming platforms to do a hybrid theatrical release. Disney+ released *Black Widow*, starring Scarlett Johansen, and it led to a contractual dispute between the studio and Johansen, who argued that she was paid less for streaming residuals than she would have received with a theatrical release. Ethics issues have come into question as studios and actors navigate the new terrain of film production that has arisen during the pandemic, which has also bled over into disputes with the studios, actors, and writers.

The rise of streaming platforms and their ability to earn coveted Academy Award nominations has leveled the playing field between the box office and streaming platforms.

Emergence of Artificial intelligence (AI)

AI has the undoubtable potential to revolutionize the way films are analyzed and studied and can potentially save studios millions of dollars in production costs. It also saves time researchers spend meticulously combing through hours of footage to identify patterns, themes, and motifs. AI can also be utilized in the creative process of filmmaking and editing itself. However, incorporating AI into filmmaking is not without its challenges.

One of the main concerns is that the filmmaking process may lose its human touch and intuition. While artificial intelligence (AI) can speed up certain areas of film analysis and production, there is a concern that depending too much on algorithms would result in formulaic and predictable films lacking the nuance and emotional depth that comes from human creativity. Finding the correct balance between using AI and keeping the human aspect will be critical for the film industry's continued success and progress.

Writer Royalties and the WGA Strike

For screenwriters, royalties are less common than fixed fees or residuals. Residuals are additional payments made when a film or TV show is rebroadcast, distributed on home video, streamed, or syndicated. The Writers Guild of America (WGA) negotiates these residuals on behalf of screenwriters. The formula for residuals can vary based on factors like the medium, the platform, and the reuse duration. The WGA provides guidelines and negotiates with producers to ensure fair compensation for screenwriters in these situations.

From May 2 to September 27, 2023, the Writers Guild of America (WGA)—representing 11,500 screenwriters—went on strike over a labor dispute with the Alliance of Motion Picture and Television Producers (AMPTP). According to online sources, one of the main focus points in the labor dispute is the residuals from streaming media; the WGA claims that AMPTP's share of such residuals has cut much of the writers' average incomes compared to a decade ago. Writers also wanted artificial intelligence, such as ChatGPT, to be used only as a tool that can help with research or facilitate script ideas and not as a tool to replace them. They highlighted these as major challenges faced by writers in the film industry, leading to massive disengagement from duties and a lower wage. This marginalization also affected the actors, leading to SAG-AFTRA joining the strike action.

SAG-AFTRA Strike

According to CBS News, the Screen Actors Guild – American Federation of Television and Radio Artists (SAG-AFTRA) is a labor union that represents approximately 160,000 media professionals and entertainers. This body represents not only actors but also journalists, talk show hosts, and other broadcast workers. Under a collective bargaining agreement spearheaded by the union, SAG-AFTRA members receive protections on pay, working conditions, and residuals. SAG-AFTRA bargains with AMPTP, representing studios, production companies, and streaming services like Paramount, Disney, and Netflix. Contracts are renegotiated every three years. While the latest contract was originally set to expire on June 30, 2023, it was extended with a new deadline: 11:59 p.m. PDT on Wednesday, July 12, 2023.

The SAG-AFTRA strike, which lasted until November 9th, 2023, focused on streaming bonuses and the indiscriminate use of artificial intelligence by these studios to replace background actors who are often paid a day rate for their work. The AI would permit the studios to use their likeness in perpetuity without hiring them for additional days of production. Background work affects not only extras but also the production crew, who spend additional days on set preparing for background scenes.

SAG-AFTRA ultimately walked away from the negotiating table with key concessions from the AMPTP, including strengthened protections around using AI and establishing a bonus based on how their work performs on streaming. The contract appears to be more of a compromise than the WGA's. It stated that actors would get a 7% raise upon the contract's ratification and then receive an additional 4% increase in the next year, totaling 11%—less than the 15% bump they initially requested. The studios and streamers also rejected SAG-AFTRA's first two proposals for new streaming compensation, with the guild settling for a bonus that will be paid out to actors on high-performing streaming shows. The Guild's president, Fran Drescher, announced that the tentative deal she negotiated for her members is worth more than $1 billion and represents "a paradigm shifts of seismic proportions."

Diversity Issues

The film industry has faced criticism for its lack of diversity in various aspects, including casting, storytelling, and behind-the-scenes roles. Advocates emphasize the need for more inclusive representation to reflect the diverse world we live in. Efforts are underway to address these issues, but progress is gradual. The film industry is dominated by White men, with Black, Asian, and Latino talent making up a much smaller percentage than their share of the total population. The lack of diverse representation is a significant obstacle for those seeking to break into the entertainment industry.

Here is the challenge: a recent study by UCLA's Center for Scholars & Storytellers found that movies that are not authentically inclusive and that have a low diversity score underperform at the box office compared to those with high diversity scores. The report analyzed over 100 films released from 2016 to 2019 and compared their earnings with their diversity scores.

They discovered that big-budget films without diverse casts earn about $27 million less at the opening weekend than those with diverse casts. This is a financial loss of $130 million throughout the movie's lifetime.

Diversity and inclusion are more than just buzzwords; they are fundamental values that should steer the film industry forward. Movies can inspire social change and build a fairer world by breaking down boundaries and embracing a diversity of opinions.

It is up to all of us—filmmakers, audiences, and activists—to make diversity and inclusion a part of the filmmaking process. Only then will we be able to really harness cinema's revolutionary power for a brighter future.

THE SHIFTING OF THE FILM MARKET

While Los Angeles remains a major player in the American film industry, there's been a gradual decentralization. The rise of streaming platforms and the ability to produce content in diverse locations have led to a dispersion of film activities. Studios and filmmakers now increasingly explore alternative regions for production, influenced by factors such as cost, tax incentives, and diverse settings. This shift reflects a broader trend in the industry's evolution beyond the traditional confines of Hollywood.

The film market shifted from Los Angeles for various reasons. One significant factor is the entertainment industry's globalization. As technology advanced, making film production more accessible globally, filmmakers started exploring diverse locations to capture unique settings and cultures. This shift allowed for a broader range of storytelling beyond the traditional Hollywood environment. Additionally, economic considerations played a role.

Filming in locations with lower production costs became attractive to studios seeking to optimize budgets. Various regions worldwide offered financial incentives, tax breaks, and lower labor costs, prompting filmmakers to consider alternatives to the higher expenses associated with Los Angeles. Furthermore, the rise of film festivals and international recognition encouraged filmmakers to explore new markets and audiences. As a result, film production expanded beyond the confines of Hollywood, contributing to the decentralization of the industry from its historical hub in Los Angeles.

The COVID-19 pandemic significantly accelerated changes in the film industry and influenced the shift in the market in several ways. The pandemic led to widespread disruptions in film production schedules. Lockdowns, travel restrictions, and safety concerns caused delays and cancellations, prompting filmmakers to reconsider traditional filming locations. Also, with theaters closing or operating at reduced capacity, there was a surge in demand for streaming services. This shift in consumer behavior elevated the importance of online platforms, encouraging filmmakers to explore non-traditional distribution models.

Pandemic restrictions forced the industry to adapt, leading to innovations in remote work and virtual production techniques. Filmmakers began considering alternative locations and decentralized production approaches, diminishing the need for a centralized hub like Los Angeles.

Moreover, travel restrictions and safety concerns led to a renewed emphasis on local and regional film productions. Filmmakers started exploring nearby locations to minimize logistical challenges and take advantage of local resources. The pandemic prompted a reassessment of production budgets and cost-effectiveness. Filming in regions with lower costs, both in terms of production and living expenses, became more appealing as the industry sought ways to recover economically.

In summary, the pandemic accelerated ongoing trends in the film industry, emphasizing the importance of flexibility, adaptability, and a global perspective. The increased reliance on streaming services and the reevaluation of traditional production methods contributed to the broader shift in the film market away from traditional centers like Los Angeles.

Technological Advancement

Technology has significantly impacted the film industry, transforming the way films are made, distributed, and consumed. In the past, making a film was a time-consuming and costly process, but with the advent of new technologies, the process has become more efficient and cost-effective.

The way we generate and consume information has altered beyond recognition in less than a decade, as has how an actor's voice, picture, or even an entire performance may be edited and reused. While streaming services and gaming provide enormous opportunities for producers and actors alike, recent technological developments pose a real threat to the integrity and economic viability of the already precarious creative professions, ranging from actors to casting directors, screenwriters, and composers.

For decades, the entertainment industry in the United Kingdom and the United States has relied on a complex and delicately balanced web of union-negotiated collective contracts, industry practice, agreed fee rates, goodwill, and negotiated deals to manage actors' performance rights (including intellectual property rights) and associated remuneration. The residuals and royalties' compensation structure, established in the 1960s, meant that performers received a regular check in the mail when content was screened, often decades after their initial performance.

In 2023, generative AI was all the trend in Hollywood. The streaming industry's structure, as well as AI's capacity to control and duplicate a performer's individually distinctive attributes, has thrown the creative world into turmoil. The repercussions, both intentional and unplanned, are immense, and the industry is becoming aware of the challenges raised by AI. They touch everything from copyright to contracts and even screenwriting and casting, as well as the bigger issue of economic fairness. The entertainment business is already transforming the way it casts and records performances thanks to generative AI. Artificial intelligence (AI) is used to analyze compatibility and on-screen attractiveness, analyzing vast datasets to identify the greatest talent to make a hit at the box office.

Furthermore, the rise of streaming services such as Netflix, Amazon Prime, Prime TV, YouTube etc., has significantly influenced the decline of traditional cable TV, with viewers able to access content on-demand. This can be done using smartphones, tablets, smart TVs, and computers, making it highly convenient.

Many streaming services offer subscription plans at a lower cost than traditional cable TV packages. Also, some streaming services like Netflix have invested heavily in producing original content, including movies, TV series, documentaries, and more. Exclusive and high-quality original content has become a major draw for subscribers, making streaming services more competitive.

The COVID-19 pandemic changed the way people consume content because of the lockdown, with a growing preference for binge-watching entire seasons or series at once. Streaming services accommodate this trend by simultaneously releasing entire seasons, which differs from the episodic nature of many cable TV shows. The improvements in internet infrastructure and the widespread availability of high-speed internet have facilitated the growth of streaming services. The ease of streaming content without the need for cable infrastructure has accelerated the shift away from traditional TV.

As a result of these factors, there has been a significant decline in cable TV subscriptions, especially among younger demographics who have embraced the convenience and variety offered by streaming between traditional cable TV and streaming services. This remains a dynamic and ongoing process.

KEY PLAYERS AND ROLES

The entertainment industry continues to evolve, as does the competition. What, then, are the key players and their roles?

THE ROLE OF BIG STUDIOS

The Role of MPAA

Founded in 1922 with major Hollywood studios coming together to form the organization called Movement Pictures Producers and Distributors of America (MPPDA), the trade association later changed its name to The Motion Picture Association., The Motion Picture Association (MPA). It was formerly known as the Motion Picture Association of America (MPAA). Major film studios in the United States are represented by MPA, which serves as a voice and advocate for them both domestically and internationally. The MPA comprises five major film production houses: Walt Disney Studios, Paramount Pictures, Warner Bros Entertainment Inc., Universal Studios, and Sony Pictures Entertainment.

One significant accomplishment attributable to this body is developing an age-based movie rating system (G, P13+, R; X rating is not commonly used).

Also, in combating piracy acts toward movies and TV shows, the advocacy work has supported members' intellectual property protection by significantly advocating copyright infringement laws besides supporting primary anti-piracy campaigns. An international presence allows it to connect governments, international organizations, and law enforcement agencies, enabling issues related to copyright protections, among others, by representing interests promoting technologies aimed at anti-authorized copying and distribution (digital rights management or DRM), protected distribution.

MPA conducts research analysis on audience demographics, trends at the box office (made by each titled story), and others. If well-informed decisions are made, due policies could positively enhance economic impacts in the sector, leading to continued growth and trajectory across the territories covered.

The film rating system is supervised by the Classification and Rating Administration (CARA), a subdivision of the MPA. Filmmakers can appeal their films' ratings before the Film and Television Ratings Appeals Board, which the MPA has nominated for this purpose.

THE ROLE OF STREAMING PLATFORMS

The American film industry has undergone a transformative shift thanks to streaming platforms. These have revolutionized content distribution, making it easy and accessible for audiences to watch films on various devices without the need for traditional theaters or TV schedules.

Leading companies such as Netflix, Hulu, Amazon Prime Video, and others are not only major players in content delivery but also produce their own films and documentaries aimed at an international audience. They challenge conventional broadcasting channels with interactive features that encourage user participation within digital communities where reviews can directly be communicated from creators.

The streaming platform's influence goes beyond consumer convenience by stirring competition among studios, which spurs innovation through increased investments and pushes a more inclusive representation of global perspectives into entertainment output.

Advancements in technology continue, partly because these alternatives support 4K streaming experiences while integrating virtual reality capabilities alongside other ideas designed around shaping immersive viewer engagements.

The film industry has witnessed a significant transformation thanks to the emergence of streaming platforms, which have introduced new possibilities and benefits. Nevertheless, these services also pose challenges that need consideration, such as revenue sharing issues, concerns over data privacy, and their impact on traditional cinemas. As things stand in this digital age where technology assumes more prominence every day, there is an ongoing shift for control between mainstream studios and online streaming providers, leading thus far toward shaping what lies ahead for American cinema's future direction.

THE ROLE OF PRODUCTION COMPANIES

Film production companies are the driving force behind the magic of cinema. They take ideas and turn them into visually stunning stories that leave lasting impressions on audiences. Their role extends beyond entertainment; they influence culture, challenge norms, and reflect the ever-evolving tapestry of human experience. As long as there are stories to tell and visions to bring to life, film production companies will continue to shape the art and culture of filmmaking, captivating audiences for generations to come. These are some of their roles:

1. Production companies are involved in the early stages of filmmaking, including developing scripts and ideas. They may acquire rights to existing material or work with writers to create original scripts for potential film projects.

2. One of the primary roles of production companies is to secure funding for film projects. This involves negotiating with investors, studios, or other financial entities to obtain the necessary resources for pre-production, production, and post-production activities.

3. Production companies are responsible for creating detailed budgets and plans for film projects. This includes allocating funds for various aspects of production, such as casting, lo-

cation scouting, set design, equipment, and post-production processes.

4. Production companies oversee the casting process, working with casting directors to select actors. They are also responsible for hiring key crew members, including the director, cinematographer, production designer, and other essential roles.

5. Production companies manage the logistical aspects of filmmaking, including scheduling, coordinating locations, and overseeing day-to-day production operations. They ensure that the production stays on schedule and within budget.

6. Production companies collaborate closely with directors, writers, and other creative professionals to bring a film's vision to fruition. This involves facilitating communication, addressing creative challenges, and providing the necessary support for the creative team.

7. Production companies handle legal aspects, including securing rights for intellectual property, negotiating contracts with talent and crew, and ensuring compliance with industry regulations and standards.

8. Mitigating risks associated with film production is a critical role of production companies. They assess potential challenges, implement strategies to address unforeseen issues and work to minimize disruptions during the production process.

9. Production companies oversee the post-production phase, which includes editing, sound design, visual effects, and other elements that contribute to the final product. They work closely with post-production teams to ensure the film meets artistic and technical standards.

10. Production companies are involved in developing distribution strategies for their films. This may involve negotiating distribution deals with studios, selecting film festivals for premieres, and planning the release strategy to reach the target audience.

11. Collaborating with marketing teams, production companies contribute to the development of promotional materials, trailers, and other marketing strategies to generate buzz and interest in the film. This is crucial for a film's success, especially during its release.
12. Production companies often submit films to prestigious film festivals as part of their distribution and marketing strategy. Success at film festivals can lead to increased visibility and recognition for the film.
13. Building and maintaining relationships within the film industry is essential for production companies. This includes relationships with talent agencies, studios, distributors, and other industry professionals.

Production companies, alongside other key players such as studios, directors, and talent agencies, contribute to the American film industry's dynamic and collaborative nature. Their role extends from the initial stages of project development to the film's release and distribution, shaping the landscape of cinematic storytelling.

THE ROLE OF MOVIE THEATER DISTRIBUTORS

Movie theater distributors play a crucial role in the competitive and dynamic American film industry by managing the distribution of films to theaters and connecting filmmakers with audiences by strategically planning and executing the distribution of films to cinemas. Their responsibilities encompass various aspects of getting films from production studios to cinema screens. Here are key aspects of the role of theater distributors:

1. Theater distributors negotiate distribution deals with production companies or studios. These deals outline the terms, conditions, and financial arrangements for the exhibition of a film in theaters.
2. Distributors decide when and where a film will be released. This involves determining the release date, selecting regions or cities for the initial release, and planning the rollout strategy to maximize audience reach.

3. Distributors provide support for marketing and promotion efforts, working with filmmakers and studios to create effective campaigns. This may include creating trailers, posters, and other promotional materials to generate buzz and interest in the film.

4. Distributors decide the number of screens (screen count) on which a film will be shown and select the theaters that will exhibit the movie. This decision is based on target audience demographics, competition, and expected box office performance.

5. Distributors manage the logistics of physically distributing film prints or, in the digital age, digital cinema packages (DCPs) to theaters. This involves coordinating the delivery and installation of prints or DCPs to ensure a smooth release.

6. Distributors negotiate revenue-sharing agreements with exhibitors (theater owners). These agreements determine how box office revenue is split between the distributor and the theater. Distributors also track box office performance and provide box office reports to filmmakers and studios.

7. Distributors coordinate the timing of a film's release across various platforms, including theatrical, home video, streaming, and television. They may manage exclusive release windows to maximize revenue across different distribution channels.

8. Building and maintaining strong relationships with exhibitors (theater owners) is crucial for distributors. This includes negotiating terms, addressing concerns, and working collaboratively to ensure successful film releases.

9. Distributors may provide support to exhibitors in terms of promotional materials, advertising support, and other incentives to encourage theaters to showcase and prioritize certain films.

10. Distributors often participate in film festivals to acquire distribution rights for promising independent films. Successful festival runs can enhance a film's marketability and visibility for a wider release.

11. With advancements in digital distribution, theater distributors have adapted to the changing landscape. They now work with digital cinema systems to deliver films in digital format, making the distribution process more efficient.
12. Distributors conduct market research to understand audience preferences and trends. This information helps them make informed decisions regarding release strategies and target demographics for specific films.
13. Theater distributors must navigate challenges such as competition from other films, seasonal fluctuations, and unexpected events that may impact a film's performance in theaters.

The film industry is an all-encompassing one. It has many interesting and lucrative fields for anyone to succeed in. Now that this chapter has opened numerous opportunities in the film industry to you, what are your interests? The next chapter may guide you even better to answer this question.

POV

Diversity

Diversity and inclusion on film sets have been a hot-button topic in the media lately. What the media doesn't tell you is the inner workings of production that may appear to be one thing on the surface, but in reality, it can be something much less complex that has perpetuated the lack of diversity in the industry.

From my experience, I was either the only person of color on set or one of the very few women who worked behind the scenes. However, over time, I came to understand that getting hired for a production is not comparable to what you would experience in a corporate work environment. There is no formal application process and usually no official posting. There is no way to quantify applicants. A lot of behind-the-scenes hiring happens over text messages and sometimes email. It's a very informal process, and it's based on relationships, referrals, and word of mouth. It all comes down to who you know and your reputation. If you don't have both components, you will hardly find enough work to supplement your expenses or maintain a decent lifestyle. This is why the film industry is elusive and hard to jump into. It's a self-sustaining environment of who you know, making it almost impossible to create a diverse environment.

The push for diversity will have to be intentional and come from the top. The executive producers must be more diverse and inclusive to bring about any real change.

AI

As someone who has worked in background casting, my initial thoughts about AI were not positive. With the recent Hollywood strikes, one of the protections that directly impact background actors is the ability for studios to use a background actor's likeness in perpetuity without having to pay that actor—who relies on a day rate. So, imagine a production would hire 200 background actors and film background scenes for two weeks. That is two weeks of employment for the background actors, casting directors, craft services, and everyone involved in a production. Without protections against using BG actors' likenesses in perpetuity, production studios are saving thousands and thousands of dollars. However, the cast and crew are losing money by the day. That is not a great way to be introduced to AI in this industry.

The first time I heard about the use of AI in the industry was after the passing of Anthony Bourdain, the beloved host of *Parts Unknown*. A released film used AI to narrate a now-deceased Bourdain into the film. The voice that was heard was eerily the same. Does a deceased person no longer have protections? It's a very grey area.

AI is currently the wild Wild West. However, there is space for AI in this industry, but with limitations. It has understandably scared many people of the potential dangers of AI mimicking voices that could lead to fraud of all kinds on behalf of unwilling participants. Still, it hasn't been all doom and gloom.

It has helped people in every industry to work more efficiently through brainstorming, writing, advice, and anything else you could think of. It has made individuals and corporations a whole lot of money. Whether you love it or hate it, AI is here to stay. We must learn to live with and regulate it to protect consumers against fraud and displacing entire industries.

Shifting film markets

As I mentioned in the preface, I came from a small town. There was no film market. If you weren't in LA, then you weren't working in the industry. Hollywood is now all across America, and that's a game-changer for aspiring filmmakers and production crews. The pandemic has only accelerated the exit from Los Angeles as production was shuttered and the cost of living sky-rocketed. Many who once had lucrative careers in the oversaturated L.A. film market have moved eastward to smaller cities with growing and fresh filmmakers.

CHAPTER TWO:
IDENTIFY YOUR TALENT AND INTERESTS

The film industry is a fun and vibrant area to explore as a potential career. While people often think of the more public professions in entertainment, like acting and directing, more jobs exist behind the scenes of a major production than are seen on a stage or film set. If you're interested in finding a job in the entertainment world or building a formidable career, finding an area you wish to develop as your expertise is important. In this chapter, I will explain how you can identify your talents and interests, offer suggestions on how to get started working in the industry, and share a list of jobs in the industry.

SELF-ASSESSMENT

Successfully identifying your area of interest in the film industry begins with making a realistic self-assessment of your talents. You should pinpoint what you are naturally good at and what people often tell you that you are good at. Sometimes, people notice things about you that you may not see in yourself. Do you like telling stories, or do you like making stories come alive? Do the characters in a book or movie intrigue you? Were you always good in English class or setting up the home entertainment system for your family?

You should sit with yourself, take notes, and reflect on what you are skilled at that you can hone in on and expand upon through practice and special courses. Do not think that you are unqualified just because you didn't attend film school or aren't fluent in film history. Believe it or not, most people in the film and TV industry never attended film school. Until you have actually worked in film production, any film theory or understanding you think you have will go out the window. You must understand that no single path leads to success, so becoming a filmmaker often requires effort put forth in unique ways.

Before you move forward with your goals to work in the film industry, it's helpful to ask yourself where you fit in the filmmaking process. Your skills and interests will certainly factor into answering this question, whether you're interested in working in one of the film crew positions, sitting on the director's chair and guiding the narrative, or standing in front of the camera as an actor. If your dream is to be the driving force behind films, you'll need to break into the filmmaking side of the industry.

Also, note that film career opportunities are wide-reaching and extensive. Some examples of jobs on a film set include casting, editing, archiving, directing, lighting, production and post-production, production design, makeup, special effects, screenwriting, sound production, and many more. Consider the various roles within the film industry and assess which roles align with your interests and passions.

Your interest in specific sectors can guide you toward roles that suit you. Do you binge reality TV shows? Are you a documentary buff and always catching the latest true-crime docu-series, or do you lean more toward narrative storytelling? Do you read more fiction or nonfiction in your spare time? Initially, you will take whatever work you are offered to get your foot in the door—but you don't want to work in a particular film genre if that's not where your passion lies. You will learn quickly that commercials pay a higher rate than reality TV shows, that reality TV shows require a lot of hand-holding of the talent, and that the scenes you see are not scripted like with narrative, but they are orchestrated by the story producer. Yes, there is a producer whose job is to create the storyline of a reality TV show.

Make It In Showbiz

Assess your technical skills related to filmmaking, such as proficiency in video editing software, camera operation, sound design, or visual effects. These skills are crucial for technical roles in the industry. You can enroll in film school or save yourself a boatload of money and sign up for a hands-on course that you can find on an e-learning platform that offers affordable training with real technicians. But remember, don't quit your day job until you get your first production job!

Apart from your technical skills, try to recognize your *creative strengths*, such as storytelling, scriptwriting, or visual aesthetics. These skills are essential for roles in writing, directing, and producing. Also, you need to evaluate your *communication skills*, as effective communication is crucial in various roles, including directing, producing, and working in post-production. Are you a collaborator and find yourself leading group projects? Are you good with finances and budgeting? Filmmaking is a collaborative effort, and strong teamwork skills are beneficial in most industry roles. If you answered yes, perhaps a role as a line producer may suit you. There is a role in filmmaking for every skill set that a person could have. You just need to find where yours fits in.

On your self-assessment journey, explore your past experiences. Reflect on any past creative group projects you were a part of. Were you into high school musicals? It could be a role you played in a high school play. The high school musical experience was a precursor for many future actors and film and live event technicians. There is also a need to consider any positive feedback, recognition, or awards you may have received for your contributions to projects, groups, or activities. These instances can highlight areas where you excel and enjoy working.

Additionally, assess how well potential film industry roles align with your values and long-term career goals. This alignment is crucial for long-term job satisfaction. Consider the impact you want to make through your work in the film industry. Whether it's telling compelling stories, influencing social change, or entertaining audiences, understanding your desired contribution can guide your career choices. If you want to settle and raise a family, you must consider that working in the industry often requires long days and nights. Most production crews work 10–14-hour days. This is not a career path where you work 9-5, Monday through Friday. The film and TV industry is not for the faint of heart. You have to be willing to work long days and many times away from home. If you are fortunate enough to live in a large production hub like Los Angeles, Atlanta, or New York, you may not have to travel too far.

You will need to develop action plans to achieve your goals, including steps for acquiring the necessary skills, building a portfolio, networking, and seeking relevant opportunities in the industry.

Note: Self-evaluation is a proactive and continuing process that allows you to better understand yourself and make more informed decisions.

This is to reiterate that you must be consistent and develop grit and mental fortitude to survive the feast or famine of cyclical production work that tends to slow down in the winter. In some months, business could be booming, and then in other months, you could be unemployed or waiting out a strike. Stay focused on your dreams and the goal because it is a process. You should seek out like-minded individuals who understand the freelance grind. It is a very lonely place, and friends and family will oftentimes question your sanity. Why would you choose to work long hours in inclement weather for minimal pay? However, if you persevere, it gets greater later. You will create freedom for yourself and an income that will help you escape the rat race and become independent, enjoying months off to travel and financial stability.

EXPLORING DIFFERENT CAREER PATHS

The American film industry offers various career paths, catering to various skills and interests. Here are some key career paths within the film industry.

1. **Director.** Directors are responsible for overseeing the creative aspects of a film. They work closely with writers, actors, and production crews to bring a script to life and ensure that the artistic vision of the project is realized.

2. **Producer.** Producers are involved in the business and logistical aspects of filmmaking. They secure funding, coordinate the production process, hire key personnel, and oversee the project from pre-production to post-production.

3. **Screenwriter**. Screenwriters are storytellers who create the script for a film. They develop the narrative, write dialogue, and collaborate with directors and producers to shape the overall storytelling structure.

4. **Cinematographer/Director of Photography (DP).** Cinematographers or DPs are responsible for capturing the visual elements of a film. They work with cameras, lighting, and composition to bring the director's vision to the screen.

5. **Film Editor.** Film editors shape the final product by selecting and arranging shots, adding sound effects, and ensuring the overall coherence of the film. They work closely with directors to achieve the desired pacing and storytelling.
6. **Production Designer.** Production designers are responsible for the overall visual look of a film. They collaborate with directors to create the aesthetic and design elements, including sets, costumes, and props.
7. **Costume Designer.** Costume designers work specifically on the wardrobe and costumes for characters in a film. They collaborate with the director and production designer to create looks that suit the characters and the story.
8. **Art Director.** Art directors are responsible for a film's visual style and aesthetics. They work closely with production designers and set decorators to ensure that the sets and locations align with the artistic vision.
9. **Sound Designer.** Sound designers are responsible for the auditory elements of a film, including dialogue, music, and sound effects. They work to enhance the overall cinematic experience through the use of sound.
10. **Composer.** Composers create a film's musical score. They work closely with directors to evoke emotions and enhance the storytelling through music.
11. **Actor.** Actors bring characters to life on screen. They work closely with directors and fellow cast members to portray roles authentically.
12. **Casting Director.** Casting directors are responsible for selecting actors for specific roles. They work closely with filmmakers to find the right talent for a film.
13. **Visual Effects (VFX) Artist.** VFX artists create computer-generated imagery (CGI) and special effects to enhance or create elements within a film. They work on everything from realistic creatures to explosive action sequences.
14. **Distribution Executive.** Distribution executives work with studios and production companies to plan the release of

films. They develop strategies for marketing and distributing films to theaters, streaming platforms, and other outlets.

15. **Film Critic/Reviewer.** Film critics analyze and review films, providing insights and opinions on their artistic and entertainment value. They may work for publications, websites, or broadcast media.

16. **Agent/Manager.** Agents and managers represent and advocate for actors, directors, writers, and other industry professionals. They help negotiate contracts, secure roles, and manage the careers of their clients.

17. **Film Festival Programmer.** Film festival programmers curate and select films for inclusion in film festivals. They are crucial in showcasing new and noteworthy films to audiences and industry professionals.

18. **Location Manager.** Location managers are responsible for scouting and securing suitable filming locations. They work with production teams to find the right places that match the script's requirements.

These are just a few examples of the diverse career paths available in the American film industry. Each role contributes uniquely to the collaborative process of bringing stories to the screen. Depending on your interests, skills, and aspirations, there are numerous opportunities for you to find a fulfilling career within this dynamic industry.

POV

Talents and interests aren't synonymous. What you are talented in isn't necessarily what you will be interested in, and vice-versa. You should be realistic with yourself. I've witnessed many people on production sets with unrealistic expectations about where they wanted to end up in the industry and what they were visibly skilled at.

There is always room to further your talent with on-the-job training. That is the best part about production. Sometimes, you go into it expecting to do one thing and come out with a completely new skill set that you are passionate about and great at. So, even when you assess your talents and skills, keep an open mind when you start your career in production. You haven't seen all the job roles and learned all the skills associated with the job. Allow yourself to be flexible in what you hope to become and enjoy the journey.

My initial goal was to become a producer. Even if I came from a performing arts background, I was realistic with myself that I did not want to be an actress. I could have perhaps been a great Taraji P. Henson or Angela Bassett (kidding), but I didn't have the passion or dedication to want to pursue it as a career. Since I knew people who were producers, I wanted to be one, too, because it seemed like a great career. All I knew was a producer worked behind the scenes and got to work first-hand with incredible talent.

I'll offer you a piece of advice. Don't just chase a title. Don't pursue things half-heartedly, even if you are decent or above average in what you are pursuing. Have you ever heard the saying, "Hard work beats talent when talent doesn't work?" Even if you are mediocre at something, if you are consistent and passionate, I believe you can master it over time and perhaps teach it to others.

After graduating from college with a degree in media communications and still having thousands of dollars in outstanding student loans, I started to investigate film school. I knew taking on more debt going to a film school was ridiculous, but I didn't care; I had that burning desire to learn more about producing. I had to find a film school in New York or Los Angeles. Those were the production hubs, and if I wasn't there and in film school, I could never learn to be a producer or make it in showbiz. Not to mention, the cost of living in both cities was outrageous then and now.

The best-accredited film schools were private institutions and very, very expensive. More expensive than my in-state tuition had been. Private loans weren't an option, and I wasn't in a financial position to pay it outright or have someone foot the bill. I was so disappointed that I figured out a plan for my life, but I didn't have the financial support to execute it. It felt like a failure. I had come so far. How could I ever be a producer if I can't even learn how to be one? There were no Masterclass series online. No affordable and easy-to-understand e-books (shameless plug).

I finally got a break soon after attending a job fair. I received my first full-time job after college as a production coordinator for a well-known international closed captioning company. I learned my technical job quickly and was good at it. I coordinated with the major networks and set up remote feeds to in-house captioners. I sat in a control room and watched captions all day for accuracy and even got to edit scripts to be caption-ready for the daytime soap opera. During the network broadcast I fed each line of captioning to TV screens across America as I listened and followed script cues. I knew what was happening daily on the *Young and the Restless* and *Days of Our Lives* because I had to read and edit the scripts each week.

This company ran 24 hours. I worked shifts that sometimes interfered with enjoying the nightlife. At 21, I was just getting a taste of being on my own and going out late-night with friends felt like freedom; I felt like I was missing out on all the fun everyone else seemed to be having.

There were times when I would leave the venue with friends at 2 am and go to work a 4 am shift. I was burning the candle at both ends. The job became monotonous, and I told myself it didn't even pay enough and that the drive was just too far outside the city. This is not how I imagined my exciting entertainment career kicking off, so I left that job after one year. That was one of the biggest mistakes I ever made on my journey.

I didn't have patience or consistency. As I stated earlier, even if you are good or mediocre at something, if you aren't passionate or consistent, the opportunity will pass you by your own doing or someone else's. If I had the opportunity to do it again, I would have stayed three years, honed in on invaluable technical skills, and used that job to relocate to a larger city at a TV network. Instead, I decided to take a sales job selling education that paid a decent salary.

I was horrible at it. Sales is where the money is at, but it's also cut-throat. You don't meet the quota, and that's it. I didn't have the gift of gab back then, so that didn't last much longer. I was starting to regret leaving my production coordinator role. Still, I had too much pride to go back and ask them to re-hire me. It was on to the next one.

Don't overlook opportunities because they aren't fun. You can't get to the top unless you pay your dues at the bottom. I was given the opportunity to skip right over being a production assistant—the lowest ranking crew on a production and became a production coordinator right out of college. A role like that takes a couple of years to get in the entertainment industry. Not to mention, no other production jobs were available in my small town. If only I had known then what I know now.

CHAPTER THREE:
RESEARCH DIFFERENT NICHES

RESEARCHING DIFFERENT GENRES

Genre Specialization and Typical Salaries

A genre is a classification or category of artistic works, such as literature, music, and films, based on shared traits, themes, and stylistic components. Genres in film help to define and recognize films with similar narrative structures, tones, and traditions. Filmmakers frequently employ genres to communicate various ideas and connect with specific audience preferences.

In the American film industry, genre specialization refers to the tendency of filmmakers, studios, or production companies to specialize in and succeed at producing films within a given genre. This specialization enables them to gain experience, appeal to a certain audience, and profit from the success of established techniques within that genre. A studio, for example, can specialize in producing horror films, romantic comedies, or action movies, becoming known for its ability to create content that meets the expectations of viewers in that genre.

Movie genres encompass a wide range of categories, each with its own distinct characteristics. Here are some major movie genres and their subgenres:

1. **Action.** Action movies are known for their high intensity, physical stunts, and intense moments. They frequently depict protagonists who face difficulties that require bravery and physical prowess, such as *The Woman King* (2022), *Sisu* (2023), and *John Wick* (2023). Subgenres in action movies are martial arts, superhero, and spy thriller.

2. **Comedy.** Comedy films aim to entertain and amuse through humor. They can range from light-hearted comedies to those with more satirical or dark humor. Subgenres in comedy are romantic comedy (rom-com), dark comedy, and slapstick. *Bridesmaids* (2011) *and Get Out* (2017) are examples of comedy movies.

3. **Drama.** Drama films focus on realistic storytelling and character development. They explore emotional themes and relationships and often depict the complexities of human experiences. Subgenres include historical drama, legal drama, and family drama. *Aviator* (2004) *and Titanic* (1997) are in this category.

4. **Horror.** Horror films aim to evoke fear and suspense in the audience. They often involve supernatural elements, psychological scares, or intense situations that create a sense of dread. Subgenres include supernatural horror, psychological horror, and slasher. *The Exorcist* (1973) and *The Conjuring* (2013) are examples of horror films.

5. **Science Fiction (Sci-Fi).** Sci-fi films explore speculative concepts often related to advanced technology, space exploration, or futuristic societies. They often push the boundaries of scientific possibilities. Subgenres include space opera, dystopian, and time travel. *Snowpiercer* (2013) and *High Life* (2019) are in this category.

6. **Fantasy.** Fantasy films feature magical elements, mythical creatures, and imaginative worlds that don't adhere to the laws of reality. They often involve epic quests and battles between good and evil. Subgenres include high fantasy, ur-

ban fantasy, and fairy tale. *Time Bandits* (1981), *Cinderella* (2015), and the *Harry Potter* series are all movies in this genre.

7. **Mystery**. Mystery films revolve around solving a puzzle or crime. They typically involve suspense, intrigue, and the gradual revelation of hidden information. Subgenres include detective, crime, and thriller. Subgenres include psychological thriller, political thriller, and conspiracy thriller. *Knives Out* (2019) and *See How They Run* (2022) are examples of mystery films.

8. **Romance**. Romance films focus on love and romantic relationships. They explore the ups and downs of love, often featuring protagonists overcoming obstacles to find happiness. Subgenres include historical romance, teen romance, and romantic drama. Have you seen the movie *Titanic*? That's a good example of a romantic movie.

9. **Adventure**. Adventure films involve exciting journeys, exploration, and often perilous quests. They can be set in various environments, from jungles to outer space. Subgenres include swashbuckler, survival, and treasure hunt. *Aquaman and the Lost Kingdom* (2023) and the *Home Alone* series are movies in this category.

10. **Western**. Westerns are set in the American Old West and often depict themes of justice, honor, and the struggle between cowboys and outlaws. *Django Unchained* (2012) and *Butcher's Crossing* (2022) describe this genre to the tee. Subgenres include classic Western and revisionist Western.

11. **Animation**. Animated films use various techniques to bring characters and stories to life through animation. They cater to a wide range of audiences and can cover diverse genres. They have become very popular in recent times despite the production cost. Subgenres include 2D animation, 3D animation, and stop-motion.

12. **Musical**. Musicals integrate songs and dance into the narrative. Characters express their emotions and advance the plot through musical numbers. Subgenres include rock musical,

dance musical, and biographical musical. The *High School Musical* series is in this category.

13. **War.** War films depict the experiences of soldiers during wartime. They can explore the harsh realities of conflict, camaraderie, and the impact of war on individuals and societies. Subgenres include war epic, and anti-war film.

14. **Documentary**. Documentaries are non-fiction films that aim to inform and educate. They cover real-world subjects, ranging from nature and history to social issues and biographies. Subgenres include nature documentary, historical documentary, and music documentary.

Many films can belong to multiple genres or subgenres, blending elements to create unique and diverse cinematic experiences. By offering a framework for expectations and preferences, genres assist both filmmakers and viewers in navigating the wide terrain of movies.

PRODUCTION POSITIONS AND TYPICAL SALARIES IN THE FILM INDUSTRY

Salaries in the film industry can vary widely based on factors such as experience, job role, overall budget, and project success. To give a typical idea of salaries, we referenced info from *Careersinfilm.com*.

- The 1st assistant director manages the schedule for a film set and coordinates all on-set departments for each shot. Salary range: $50,000 to $75,000.
- The 2nd assistant camera works on the camera team, organizing lenses, building camera gear, and running the slate. Salary range: $42,000 to $62,000.
- The 2nd assistant directors help the assistant director to ensure a set runs smoothly. This may include tracking progress on schedule, creating call sheets, working with extras, etc. Salary Range: $64,000 to $121,000.
- An actor embodies a character in a film, TV show, or other type of content. With research of that character, memorization of dialogue, and collaboration with the director of the project. Salary range: $15,500 to $139,500.
- ADR mixers correct dialogue and sound issues in the original production. They remove background noise, re-record dialogue with lip-synching, and clean up production audio. Salary range: $51,000 to $114,000.
- An armorer supervises the use of all weapons on a film set and provides instruction for the actors on how to use them properly and safely. Salary range: $12,000 to $88,000.
- An art director oversees the building of sets and the creation of all show signage in line with the vision of the production designer. Salary range: $50,000 to $112,000 (on lower budget projects, these roles may be combined).
- An assistant costume designer helps costume designers with all looks for actors on set. They also plan, create, organize, and help maintain clothes on set. Salary range: $25,000 to $100,000.
- An assistant editor supports the main Picture Editor by preparing projects, cleaning up timelines and handling exports. Salary range: $39,000 to $87,000.
- An assistant makeup artist can do everything from natural beauty to turning a person into a literal monster. They may also be in charge of body makeup, organization, or keeping actors looking perfect. Salary range: $16,000 to $36,000.

- Whereas the production accountant takes care of macro-level financials and overall budgets for a production, the assistant production accountant takes care of micro-level financials. Salary range: $38,000 to $77,000.
- An assistant Production Coordinator problem-solves every aspect of production. Their countless responsibilities include being the main point of contact for everyone on set, distributing scripts, and coordinating production. Salary range: $40,000 to $70,000.
- An assistant property master assists the prop master with anything actors handle on set. They ensure the correct props are prepared, on hand for the shoot, and archived once a scene is wrapped. Salary range: $31,000 to $64,000.
- An associate producer (AP) assists in putting a production together. This nuts-and-bolts position may include writing, editing, organizing, and assisting various crew members in pulling off their roles to details. Salary range: $40,000 to $105,000.
- The Best Boy is the title given to the head assistant to the gaffer or key grip in their respective departments. Average salary: $92,000.
- A boom operator places and holds the boom microphone to record the dialogue for actors during a film or television shoot. They need to know the basics of the use of wireless microphones. Salary range: $37,000 to $121,000.
- A casting assistant holds a largely administrative role in the casting process. They report to and support casting directors. They work with actors' schedules, schedule auditions, and construct casting. Salary range: $42,000 to $81,000.
- A casting associate assists in the casting of actors in film and television. Salary range: $41,000 to $105,000.
- A casting director helps directors and producers find the right Actors for their film, TV, and commercial productions. Salary range: $69,000 to $110,000.

- A choreographer devises dance routines for film, TV, and commercial productions. They also teach the moves to dancers and actors on set. Salary range: $38,000 to $61,000.
- A cinematographer works with the director to achieve the overall visual aesthetic of a film, television show, commercial, music video, or other type of content. Average salary: $83,500.
- A co-producer coordinates the different production departments and logistical needs of the production team. Salary range: $43,000 to $158,000.
- A colorist is a post-production professional who processes every image in a cinematic production to achieve a desired visual look. The work is a sort of hybrid of visual effects and cinematography. Salary range: $700 to $1,000 a day.
- A company producer works within a specific department in the different post-production houses to coordinate and manage schedules for the sound, color, visual effects, or editing talent. Salary range: $70,000 to $100,000.
- A composer creates the score for a motion picture by writing, revising, and recording new music to elicit an emotional response. Salary range: $42,000 to $59,000.
- A costume designer creates the costumes that help to inform the characters and tell their stories in a film. They are the artistic head for all costume-based decisions on a shoot. Salary range: $3,000 to $3,500+ per week on a film.
- A digital imaging technician is responsible for wrangling all data on set and duplicating it for safety. They're responsible for ensuring all footage is available and intact for the editor. Salary range: $250,000 to $750,000 per day, plus gear.
- A director is the storyteller in charge of every creative aspect, from development to post-production. They ensure that the film's story is conveyed through the actors' performances. Salary range: $250,000 to $2,000,000.
- A director of photography or DP works with a director to execute their vision for the script. They are in charge of both

the camera and lighting departments, creating the visuals that help tell the story. Average salary: $83,500.

- A dolly grip prepares a location or set for camera motion and supports the camera any time it is moving. They lay protective flooring according to the scene and hold the camera. Salary range: $100,000 to $300,000.
- A drone operator works to remotely pilot an aircraft to get footage from above a specific location during production. Salary range: $39,000 to $92,000.
- An executive producer provides the financial backing for a film project. Their involvement depends on the project, with some EPs only securing funds and others getting involved in the filmmaking. Salary range: $109,000 to $200,000.

Please note that the roles in the film industry are not limited to those listed above. As you can see, once you reach a level of mastery, you become the master of your destiny. Your work and experience will speak for itself.

FILM FESTIVALS AND INDEPENDENT MOVIES

Film festivals are gatherings that present a selection of films to a live audience, sometimes organized by genre, topic, or geographic origin. These festivals range from small, local gatherings to massive, worldwide gatherings. Film festivals' primary objectives include:

1. **Screening Films.** Film festivals show a carefully chosen collection of films, which may include feature films, documentaries, short films, and experimental works. The purpose is to show viewers a varied spectrum of cinematic productions.
2. **Promoting Filmmakers.** Festivals give a venue for filmmakers to present their work and earn visibility. This exposure may lead to distribution deals, recognition, and future project chances.
3. **Awards and Recognition.** Many film festivals have competitions in which films are assessed and awards given out in categories such as Best Film, Best Director, Best Actor, and

others. Winning awards at prestigious film festivals may considerably boost a filmmaker's profile.
4. **Networking.** Film festivals bring together filmmakers, industry executives, reviewers, and fans for networking. This setting encourages networking by connecting filmmakers with possible partners, distributors, and other significant individuals in the film business.
5. **Cultural Exchange.** International film festivals frequently feature films from around the world, encouraging cultural exchange and giving viewers a glimpse into diverse societies, views, and storytelling traditions.
6. **Educational Programs.** Workshops, panel talks, and Q&A sessions with filmmakers are all part of certain festivals' educational programs. These initiatives benefit both filmmakers' and viewers' educational and professional growth.

Well-known film festivals include the Tribeca Int'l Film Festival, Hamptons Intl Film Festival, Cannes Film Festival, Sundance Film Festival, Berlin International Film Festival, and Toronto International Film Festival, among others. These events attract attention from the global film industry and play a crucial role in shaping the trajectory of films and filmmakers.

INDEPENDENT FILMS

Independent films, sometimes known as indie films, are created independently of big film studios. These films are distinguished by a lesser budget, directors' creative freedom, and a focus on artistic expression and unique narrative. Independent films can span a wide range of genres and issues, frequently exploring stories that do not meet conventional commercial expectations.

Notable independent filmmakers and directors often associated with this genre include Quentin Tarantino, Richard Linklater, Sofia Coppola, and Spike Lee. Independent movies have made significant contributions to the art of filmmaking by challenging conventions and offering alternative narratives to audiences.

POV

Niche is quite the buzzword these days. You absolutely should do your research, just like I did my research on what a producer was. I knew nothing about budgets, location agreements, contracts, releases, negotiating, etc.

One of the biggest niches in production is craft services, aka "crafty." They provide all cast and crew with breakfast, lunch, snacks, and catered dinners on set. You will want for nothing. You will never need to spend money on food, and this is great if you are a production assistant and on a shoestring budget.

I can't even remember the number of times I came home with garbage bags full of fruit snacks, LaCroix water, and random food and snacks. Don't be so obvious that you are scouring crafty for leftovers. Wait until the day is at an end and the production has wrapped. That's when they realize they don't want to waste to make productions more "green"—as in environmentally friendly.

Production assistants are crucial to every production. However, they are often seen as paying their dues. They are errand runners and receive the least amount of pay. After 1-2 years of working as a production assistant, you must find a way to advance into a niche in which you've found interest and enjoyment or pick the management track. Otherwise, you risk burnout and being broke.

When you advance to the next level, new roles open up into jobs like camera assistant, production coordinator and production manager. That's when your rates go up, and you move beyond your feast or famine days. As your name starts to matriculate through the industry, you no longer have to feverishly search websites like Mandy or Staff Me Up.

To be honest, I have been hired from Staff Me Up once. That's how essential building your network on each production gig is. Staff Me Up is still a necessary evil. Don't waste your money on the paid membership. However, you still need to be visible on Staff Me Up for the simple fact that it's a great way to connect with people who have worked for the same networks and production companies and keep a track record of your film credits and job titles. You may need them for later reference when you decide if you want to join the union. You'll also want to use your credits to build your IMDb page. Once you are on IMDb, you have arrived. Well, that's how it felt for me. Look up your favorite producers, directors, and actors, and you'll see that every project they have ever touched is listed in this global movie database. Yours will be too.

After working on gigs consistently for a year, you will have built a network of associates who will refer you for gigs if they are already booked, want to work with you again, or have moved into a more senior role and know you're reliable. I got my first gig as a talent coordinator from a former associate who was hired on the project, and he shot me a text message saying, "Hey, are you available for work? We need a talent coordinator for this gig that's in town." Most times, it happens just like that. Your reputation on set and the connections you build follow you onto every production and determine whether you will be booked or busy. My most recent casting job was an Oscar-winning film that came through a referral from a 1st AD (assistant director) who had worked with me previously and recommended me to a casting director.

Keep in mind production gigs are not all created equal. From my perspective, working commercial gigs were the most desired because they typically paid significantly more than the average day rate and had the least amount of shoot days. You could make in 3 days what it would take a week to make on a reality show gig.

This brings me to working on reality TV-based programming. This was my least desired opportunity, but they were more abundant, had longer shoot periods, and provided more consistency. Even with reality-based TV gigs, there were levels. Working for a channel like the History Channel or TLC usually had a robust budget, was well-organized, and professional. Nothing exciting, but it paid the bills.

Then, you have your reality shows that often break out into fights and involve a lot of babysitting on set. That happens because these aren't professional actors or experts in their fields like in a docuseries. Sometimes, you become a surrogate friend, family member or therapist just to get people ready to shoot on location. This led to longer production days and delays.

Even though reality shows aren't scripted, they still have storylines. A producer teases the story for the overall series or episode and sometimes prompts the talent to elaborate or take situations in a certain direction. It can be fun but a nightmare if you have unruly or demanding talent. You want them to "perform," and they want to know what's in it for them. This can put major constraints on the production budget, from lavish hotel stays to expensive dinners and extremely late call times. If you are brave enough to stay in reality TV, get out of the production assistant role as soon as possible. You could work your way into a story producer role within a few years. When you book a series as any type of production manager and above the line roles like producer, you are booked for the whole season. This is great because you can now receive a weekly rate instead of a day rate, which brings consistency, and production covers your travel and food per diems.

CHAPTER FOUR:
CREATE YOUR UNIQUE BRAND

In this chapter, we'll look at developing your style, creating an online portfolio highlighting your skills, and building a strong online presence for effective networking. These crucial components are necessary for anyone navigating the shifting environment of the entertainment industry, letting you stand out and leave a lasting impression on your route to showbiz success.

DEVELOPING YOUR STYLE

For you to successfully create your niche and stand out in the ever-competitive industry, you need to create your uniqueness and authenticity by developing your style. Developing your distinctive style in the film industry is a process that combines self-discovery, artistic research, and a commitment to authenticity. Here are some methods to help you:

1. **Investigate Influential Filmmakers.** Analyze the works of filmmakers who inspire you. Find out their storytelling strategies, visual aesthetics, and thematic features. Use this information to help you establish your own style.
2. **Experiment With Different Genres.** Research a range of film genres thoroughly to see what speaks to you. Experi-

menting with different techniques will help you discover your interest, unique voice, and storytelling approach.

3. **Identify Your Themes and Motifs.** Reflect on the themes and motifs that consistently interest you. Whether it's exploring human relationships, societal issues, or specific emotions, identifying your recurring interests contributes to the coherence of your style.

4. **Accept Your Point of View.** Your experiences and points of view are great assets. Accept them and allow them to impact your storytelling. Authenticity is frequently derived from a true connection to the material presented.

5. **Continuity Between Projects.** Strive for consistency in your style between projects. This does not imply stagnation but rather a recognized thread connecting your body of work.

You must always remember that establishing your style is a never-ending process. It changes as you develop emotionally and professionally. Accept the learning process, remain curious, and let your distinct perspective shine through in your film projects.

Building an Online Portfolio

Portfolios are collections of your work, either in the form of a website or a physical artist's case. For many roles in the screen industries, it's essential to have a portfolio that demonstrates your creativity. Your portfolio is undoubtedly your most valuable asset as a filmmaker.

A well-structured portfolio showcases your technical ability while also telling a fascinating story about your artistic path and vision. That is why devoting time and effort to creating a portfolio that reflects your passion and devotion is a necessary step toward success. Creating an online portfolio entails numerous stages. Here's a quick start guide to get you started.

1. **Define Your Goal.** Clearly define the goal of your portfolio. What's the purpose of the portfolio? What niche am I going into? Who is my target audience? Are you displaying a vid-

eo sizzle reel of your projects, writing scripts, or graphic designs for movie posters?

2. **Select a Platform**. You will always need a steady online presence, so choose between using a website builder (such as Wix, Squarespace, or WordPress), portfolio-specific platforms (Behance or Dribble), or creating a custom website.

3. **Get a Custom Domain Name.** If possible, get a custom domain name (www.yourname.com). It gives your portfolio a professional appearance.

4. **Choose a Clean Template or Theme**. Select a template or theme that is consistent with your work and easy to browse. Choose a simple and professional design.

5. **Make Sections**. Make sections for your portfolio, such as Home, About Me, Work/Projects, Resume, and Contact. Make it simple for visitors to navigate.

6. **Page About Yourself.** Create a succinct and interesting "About Me" section. Highlight your abilities, experience, and what distinguishes you.

7. **Portfolio Section**. Display your best work in a visually pleasing way. Include project descriptions, pictures, and any other pertinent information. If applicable, organize comparable work into categories.

8. **Resume/CV.** Consider adding a downloadable version of your resume or CV. Make it easily accessible for potential employers or clients.

9. **Contact Information**. Display your contact details clearly. You may include a contact form for inquiries.

10. **Optimize for SEO.** To boost search engine exposure, use important keywords in your content. This is necessary so that future clients or employers can locate you.

11. **Mobile-Friendly.** Test it on several devices to ensure a consistent user experience.

12. **Social Media Integration.** Include connections to your professional social media platforms. This can help with networking and provide more insight into your professional persona.

13. **Test and Review.** Thoroughly test your portfolio before releasing it. Examine the site for broken links, typos, and overall functionality.
14. **Launch Your Portfolio.** Once satisfied with the design and content, publish your portfolio.
15. **Regular Updates.** Keep your portfolio up to date. Add new projects, update your resume, and make any necessary changes to reflect your current status and achievements.
16. **Testimonials and Recommendations**. If applicable, include testimonials or recommendations from clients or collaborators. This adds credibility to your work.
17. **Legal Considerations**. If you're using music or any copyrighted material in your films, ensure you have the right permissions or licenses. Clearly mention any collaborations or partnerships.
18. **Promote Your Portfolio.** Share your portfolio on social media, filmmaking forums, and other relevant platforms. Actively promote your work to increase visibility.
19. **Portfolio Review**. Ask for feedback from peers or mentors. Constructive criticism can help you improve your portfolio's overall presentation and content.
20. **Stay Updated**. Stay informed about industry trends and update your portfolio accordingly. This demonstrates your commitment to growth and improvement.

Remember that your online portfolio and social media presence are a dynamic reflection of your skills and knowledge. They will continue to be a great tool for advertising your work and building connections if regularly updated and improved.

ONLINE PRESENCE AND NETWORKING

As it continues to be an important part of our lives, social media impacts every industry, including filmmaking. Traditional approaches such as film festivals and word-of-mouth promotion are no longer sufficient for a successful film career.

Today, a large portion of its success is determined by whether the internet jury thinks it is worthy of praise and virality. That is why filmmakers (and even huge production companies) are implementing a social media strategy into their marketing tactics to engage with their audience and build a dedicated global fanbase that will support new film releases.

Social media has transformed how filmmakers communicate with their audiences, peers, and even investors, making it a powerful networking, audience engagement, and crowdfunding platform.

Online social platforms enable filmmakers to network and market their work for free. Filmmakers can readily contact other industry experts, including producers, agents, and casting directors, using these channels. Such relationships can lead to new employment prospects, such as being hired for a project or working on a new film with other professionals. They can even use social media to increase their fan base and boost their following.

Furthermore, filmmakers use social media as part of their marketing plan to promote their work to a wider audience. They may promote their films, trailers, and behind-the-scenes content through their internet profiles and reach many people quickly.

Connecting with other professionals in the industry—be it executives, directors, screenwriters, producers, or actors—enables filmmakers to expand their network, learn from others, and potentially open up new opportunities for collaboration and growth. This is one way to leverage your online presence to build your network base. Interacting with them online is a good way to start since it's relatively easy and doesn't usually require a formal introduction. Doing so not only allows filmmakers to establish a good connection with industry professionals but can also help them gain new supporters and online traffic as the audience of the person they are connecting with takes an interest in them. Remember, networking is about building relationships, not just accumulating connections. Actively engage, support others, and contribute to your professional community to create a meaningful online presence.

POV

When people think of branding, they think of big corporations with professional logos and matching colors. Branding can also apply to how you present yourself and want others to see you—standing out in a sea of people who are probably just as eager as you.

One of the first things I did after my first gig was to make a business card. After my first gig I couldn't remember anyone I had networked with. Luckily, I still had emails and call sheets for reference. So, for my next gig, I was more prepared. It was a simple white card with big black lettering. It had my first and last name, my email and said something like "Available for Work." I also created a website page using my first and last name. This website has evolved over the years. As you gain more experience, keep your website up to date. Whenever anyone googles your name, that's the first thing that comes up.

Set yourself apart with your professionalism and set etiquette. Always be prepared on set and dressed appropriately.

The best way to show up is by wearing comfortable clothing, sneakers, hair pulled back, and a fanny pack with essentials. Think about the things that those in various departments may need on set. People will start to see you as the go-to person for essential but random things. Examples of what to keep in your pack are Ibuprofen, safety pins, tape, bandaids, tissue, hand sanitizer and, of course, your networking business card. That fanny pack will set you apart.

When you build rapport with folks in various departments, let them know after filming wraps to shoot you an email if they ever need assistance on set. Don't just shove your card onto people. Do it organically and genuinely. People love to consistently work around people they can depend on. Most of the industry is built on a referral system. If you build your referral system one by one on each gig, you will have a Rolodex in your phone of producers and production managers who will come looking for you—mostly in the form of a simple text. Sometimes, with just a few days notice.

One of the things I did was a bit egoistic, but it was to help promote myself for more opportunities. This was very uncomfortable for me initially, but I had to learn to leverage social media to show those who looked me up that I was landing high-profile gigs and get them excited about working with me. You never want to take pictures of celebrity talent on set. That is a huge no-no, and it just makes you look starstruck. For that reason, you will often have to sign an NDA to work on a production. However, I found ways on set to still take pictures covertly of myself engaged in production work. It could have been a picture of me assisting the costumer with wardrobe or driving a production van. I wanted to showcase myself in various settings to show that I could function in multiple departments and was an invaluable production assistant. A series of film-related hashtags followed a post on my social media channel. To create my brand, I was curious, go-getting, problem-solving, and chronically on time.

There's a saying in production, "If you're on time, you're late–if you're early, you're on time." I lived by this. I made it a point to arrive at my call time 20-30 minutes beforehand. Always make punctuality a part of your unique brand. Starting after the crew call means a delay in filming and pushes the entire shooting schedule back. That's bad news for producers and executive producers because it affects their bottom line. It leads to meal penalties for production and potential overtime for union labor. If you plan to take the management track in production, this will be essential to being a good coordinator or production manager who can avoid excessive spending from the production budget because of lateness.

Building my unique brand was a combination of skills, personal presentation, and personality. It's evolved over the years as I've gained more experience. I made it a point to be friendly and smile often. Working in production can be intense, and you'll meet a lot of unfavorable personalities who want to project onto you. You have to learn not to internalize the behaviors of others and understand they're not a reflection of you or your capabilities.

Sometimes, people bring their dramas and traumas to work, resulting in a bad day for everyone around them. Seeing a smiling face can spark conversation and change the energy in a toxic environment. Eventually, you'll get noticed by someone above you.

Not everyone possesses people skills. I happened to have them, and even though I was more of an introvert, I enjoyed talking to people one-on-one. Because of my personality, my gigs started to evolve into roles that had to interact directly with talent.

CHAPTER FIVE:

NAVIGATING THE COMPETITIVE LANDSCAPE

Professionals attempting to make a name for themselves in the ever-changing world of the industry, where creativity meets business, face a challenging and rewarding landscape. In this chapter, we'll look at crucial aspects of navigating this competitive climate, such as identifying possibilities and difficulties, techniques for finding jobs or freelancing, and the critical importance of networking.

IDENTIFYING OPPORTUNITIES AND THREATS

The American film industry, often recognized as a global leader in cinema, is characterized by its ever-evolving environment. Understanding the opportunities and threats within this dynamic sector is crucial for upcoming talents or professionals aiming to go through and succeed in the industry. Let's view some of the opportunities and challenges below.

Opportunities

1. **Emerging Technologies.** Virtual reality (VR) and augmented reality (AR), for example, give new avenues for presenting tales and engaging audiences. Filmmakers and content providers can experiment with these technologies to better their viewers' cinematic experiences while also tapping into changing consumer preferences.
2. **Diverse Storytelling.** There is a growing need for films that represent a diverse spectrum of voices and perspectives, as

there is an increasing emphasis on diversity and inclusion. This allows filmmakers to explore fresh storylines and contribute to the industry's more inclusive community.

3. **Streaming Platforms**. The rise of streaming services has disrupted traditional distribution models. As much as this might seem like a challenge, however, filmmakers now have the opportunity to create content for platforms like Netflix, Hulu, and Disney+, providing a broader reach and alternative distribution channels outside of traditional theaters. It is less expensive and thus more cost-effective.

4. **International Collaboration**. Collaborating with international filmmakers and accessing global markets has become more feasible with the presence of social media platforms. This presents opportunities for cross-cultural exchange, co-productions, and reaching diverse audiences worldwide. A rising filmmaker can harness this opportunity.

Threats

1. **Piracy and Copyright Issues**. The digital age brings the challenge of piracy, impacting revenue streams for filmmakers. Protecting intellectual property and combating piracy remain ongoing challenges for the industry. You must consider this and how you can protect yourself from this or proffer a solution for the industry.

2. **Changing Consumer Behavior.** Shifts in consumer behavior, such as a preference for streaming over traditional cinema, can pose challenges for filmmakers and distributors. Adapting to these changes and finding innovative ways to capture audience attention are critical for film producers today. You must be ready to cater to the needs of your audience.

3. **Budget Constraints.** While technology opens new possibilities, it also comes with costs. High production budgets, marketing expenses, and the competitive nature of the industry can lead to financial challenges, especially for independent filmmakers.

4. **Regulatory Challenges.** The film industry operates within a regulatory framework that can impact content creation and

distribution. Changes in regulations, censorship issues, or rating restrictions may pose challenges for filmmakers.

To summarize, navigating the American film industry necessitates an acute awareness of emerging opportunities as well as prospective challenges. This will assist you in adapting to advancements in technology, embracing varied narrative approaches, and addressing difficulties strategically.

STRATEGIES FOR GETTING HIRED OR FREELANCING IN THE AMERICAN FILM INDUSTRY

The biggest hurdle getting into the industry after doing all of the above is actually landing your first job. It becomes an uphill battle if you don't have the experience, haven't gone to film school, and have done all of your networking. Some programs are tailored to train aspiring technicians how to land that first job. These programs can cost upwards of $5,000. Save your money and take online courses and webinars. Workshops, e-learning, networking and on-the-job training will land you your first production gig. There are strategies that you must implement continuously to stay on top of your game. This is because the American film industry is known for its competitiveness and creative demands. Therefore, individuals seeking employment or freelancing opportunities must be proactive and strategic in their pursuit.

Most job hires in the industry come from recommendations of your peers, not from a job board on LinkedIn. Often, it will be as informal as a text message that reads, "Hey, John gave me your number. We'll be shooting there for two weeks next month. Are you available for work?" It's all about who you know and the reputation you've built for yourself by being consistent and skilled. To land your first production gig, there are several angles that you should take all at once.

1. **Contact the Local Film Office.** Consider the market that you are in. Research online about your city and state's film office. The film office is responsible for granting productions access to film on location and providing them with tax credits. Usu-

ally, the film office will have a listing of all production crew, vendors, and upcoming film projects in your city. Make sure you are on the crew list as a production assistant.

2. **Build a List of Local Film Festivals.** Also, find out what film festivals are closest to you, even if you must travel a few states over. Be willing to work as a volunteer if there are no paid opportunities. Most film festivals are run by volunteers and paid staff. Make a list of all the film festivals that interest you so that you can also work as a local. Identify when the festival dates are, and 4-6 months out, check their websites for job openings. All you need is just one to get started. This will lead you to connect with professionals in the film industry very quickly. Participating in filmmaker panels at those festivals is a great way to learn about the best in the industry while also being on staff and getting paid.

3. **Crafting a Standout Portfolio.** You have to start by developing a comprehensive and diverse portfolio that shows your range of skills. Include projects that highlight your proficiency in different genres, styles, and aspects of filmmaking, whether it's directing, cinematography, editing, or other roles. You must also prioritize quality over quantity when selecting projects for your portfolio. Showcase projects that demonstrate your ability to tell compelling stories, handle technical challenges, and contribute creatively to a production.

4. **Gaining Hands-on Experience.** As you enter the industry for the first time, seek internships or entry-level positions to gain practical experience. Working on film sets, even in minor roles, provides valuable insights into production dynamics and allows you to build connections with professionals in the field. This enabled you to use every opportunity to network while working on projects. Collaborate with colleagues, express your enthusiasm, and establish relationships with individuals who can potentially open doors to future opportunities.

5. **Staying Updated on Industry Trends.** Be a lifelong learner. Stay abreast of industry trends, emerging technologies, and new storytelling techniques. Attend workshops, take cours-

es, and participate in industry events to expand your knowledge and skill set. Also, given the dynamic nature of the film industry, being adaptable is crucial. Be open to learning new tools and techniques, as well as staying informed about changes in distribution models and audience preferences.

6. **Leveraging Online Platforms**. As mentioned earlier, you must establish a strong online presence through platforms like LinkedIn, Vimeo, or personal websites. Showcase your portfolio, share insights about your work, and connect with industry professionals. Online visibility can attract attention from potential employers or collaborators.

7. **Freelancing Platforms**. You can also choose to explore freelancing platforms specific to the film industry, where filmmakers and production companies post opportunities for various roles. Platforms like Mandy, Production Beast, or Staff Me Up can be valuable resources for finding freelance gigs.

8. **Networking With Industry Professionals**. The need to network cannot be overemphasized regarding making it in the film industry. You will need to invest in attending film festivals, industry conferences, and networking events. These gatherings provide opportunities to meet established professionals, exchange ideas, and potentially secure projects or collaborations. You can also reach out to professionals for informational interviews. It will serve as a medium to learn about their experiences, seek advice, and express your interest in the industry. Building genuine connections can lead to mentorship or job referrals.

In conclusion, a multidimensional approach that includes a standout portfolio, hands-on experience, constant learning, internet presence, and successful networking is critical for anyone seeking employment or freelance opportunities in the American film industry.

THE IMPORTANCE OF NETWORKING

Like many other professional spheres, the entertainment industry is built on a complicated web of relationships, and appreciating the value of these ties is frequently the key to unlocking the right doors of opportunity. The economy is changing, and the way people work is changing along with it.

In a collaborative industry, it's not just about who you know but who knows you. Every audition, screenplay reading, or fortuitous meeting at a social gathering could lead to future opportunities or collaborations. Building true relationships with casting directors, producers, fellow performers, and other industry professionals provides a safety net. When someone speaks up for an associate's talent or work ethic, they are more likely to be considered for gigs. Furthermore, established connections can provide guidance, mentorship, and even financial support for independent projects.

Networking in the film industry is a path to building lasting relationships. It's about more than going to the right parties, shaking hands, and smiling. Successful film networking is a combination of trying networking tools, finding the right opportunities, and finding a balance between what you need and what you can offer.

Also, networking exposes you to opportunities that may not be publicly advertised. Through conversations and connections, you may learn about upcoming projects, auditions, or positions that align with your skills and aspirations. Furthermore, the film industry can be demanding and unpredictable. Networking allows you to connect with individuals who understand the unique challenges, providing emotional support during both highs and lows.

Finally, networking is not just a means to an end in the film industry; it is an ongoing and integral part of professional development. Building and nurturing relationships within the industry contributes not only to individual success but also to the overall vibrancy and collaborative spirit that defines filmmaking.

POV

Navigating the competitive landscape goes beyond the complexities of the film industry itself. It also touches upon how you will interact with others within the industry. I went into production very "green." Green is what they call you when you are new to working behind the scenes. My personality is very bubbly and friendly but also introverted. I am not aggressive, but I tend to lead when I see the need. I am what you would call a sigma.

Sigmas are lone wolves that possess quiet strength. They appear shy, analyze everything around them, and communicate in smaller group settings. They don't attempt to be the most noticed or the loudest in the room. They keep their head down and let the work speak for them. They will roll up their sleeves, get the job done, and expect you to do the same. Sometimes, people will take the more reserved, quiet, and hardworking person as an easy target for exploitation. This exploitation can look like taking credit for your work, verbal abuse, devaluing, gaslighting, leaving you to do menial tasks with no regard to your time and picking up the slack of others while paying you less than the team around you. You will recognize it when it happens because it pulls at your soul.

You're always agreeable, available, and hard-working. These virtuous qualities will not help you elevate to the next level quickly. You will work with different personality types working in entertainment. I've watched people who were inexperienced, inefficient, and unorganized but had dominant personalities move up the ranks with ease. The most authoritarian people take off fast out the gate. You have to learn your boundaries, be assertive, and never deviate from that.

Remember this is a marathon, not a sprint. You risk burning out coming out the gate too fast. Assertive and authoritative are different ends of the same spectrum. Assertive is when you roll up your sleeves and lead by example. Authoritative leadership means you give orders but never do the work or show others the blueprint of how it should be done. In addition, authoritative leadership tends to instill fear in those in a lesser role. I prefer to be assertive and have the respect of my team over authoritative and instilling fear. Fear can only go so long and breeds contempt. You have to decide the kind of colleague and eventual leader you want to be in the industry.

When you are respected, people will trust that you will always be fair in your decision-making, even if it provides a less-than-favorable outcome. It took me a very long time to understand how I was easily exploited early on because I thought being a kind person was enough.

The moment I became assertive and placed boundaries in my personal and professional life, everything changed for me. I also didn't have to change being the bubbly, optimistic person I had always been. I learned to turn it on like a light switch. People will test your boundaries, and you'll have to respectfully introduce them to your "representative".

Many people have had to compromise their values to move up the ranks, and they will expect the same from you. There are toxic personality types in every industry. They just seem to run a bit more rampant in entertainment.

Take time to assess your own personality type and leadership style. Many personality tests online, like the Myers-Briggs personality test, can unveil who you really are at your core. It will also tell you what professions and skill sets complement your personality type. It's often hard to see ourselves the way others perceive us because we don't practice self-awareness or have a low emotional intelligence. Emotional intelligence is the capacity to be aware of, control, and express one's emotions and handle interpersonal relationships judiciously and empathetically.

Personality tests can bring self-awareness to your weakest traits so you can turn them into strengths. For me, it was learning to be assertive and having proper boundaries. Do yourself and everyone around you on a production a favor and learn who you are and develop your emotional intelligence before you think about leading or working alongside anyone, anywhere.

CHAPTER SIX:
SKILLS, CERTIFICATIONS, AND EDUCATION

In the fast-paced realm of the American film industry, success is frequently defined as a combination of natural talent and the strategic acquisition of skills, qualifications, and education. From the necessary abilities needed by filmmaking's creative and technical aspects to the key decision of pursuing formal education or on-the-job training, this chapter provides you with the knowledge required to traverse the film industry's varied landscape.

RELEVANT CERTIFICATIONS: GOING TO FILM SCHOOL VS. ON-THE-JOB TRAINING

Relevant certifications in the film industry validate your skills and knowledge, giving employers confidence in your abilities. Credibility is added to your resume because you have recognized certifications that demonstrate a commitment to professional development. Also, certification programs often connect you with industry professionals and peers, expanding your network. Some certifications provide access to specialized resources, equipment, or communities that can enhance your filmmaking capabilities.

Furthermore, having certifications in a competitive industry can set you apart from other candidates, potentially increasing job opportunities. Film schools offer these certifications to individuals.

However, film school can be expensive, and success in the film industry often relies on practical experience. Some argue that self-learning and networking can be equally valuable without the financial burden of formal education. Additionally, the industry values a strong portfolio and connections as much as or more than a degree.

There has been a lot of argument centered around the profitability of going to a film school to get certifications or just having on-the-job training. This is because not everyone in the film industry went to film school. There are, in fact, numerous successful directors who never received formal training—including James Cameron, Quentin Tarantino, Paul Thomas Anderson, and David Fincher.

The film industry wants people with prior experience and contacts, while degrees and diplomas are of limited importance. While most film schools can teach the technical and practical skills required, many do not offer students the opportunity to obtain work experience or build direct relationships inside the business. Those who avoided film school found other ways to educate themselves and made the necessary connections to get in the door. As a result, many film school graduates have no employment prospects, and many never receive one. Moreso, on-the-job training often offers a more direct path to understanding the dynamics of filmmaking and can be a cost-effective alternative to formal education.

Now that you know the advantages and disadvantages of going to a film school and on-the-job training, the decision lies with you to make the best choice for a career in the industry.

ESSENTIAL EDUCATION AND COURSES

While the film industry often values practical experience and a strong portfolio, certifications can still enhance your credentials. Consider these types of certifications relevant to the American film industry:

1. **Avid Certification.** Avid is widely used in film editing. Certifications like Avid Certified User or Avid Certified Professional can demonstrate proficiency in editing software.

2. **Final Cut Pro Certification.** If you're focusing on Apple's Final Cut Pro, becoming a certified user or pro can showcase your expertise in this editing platform.
3. **Screenwriting Software Certification.** Certifications in popular screenwriting software like Final Draft or Celtx can validate your skills in scriptwriting.
4. **Cinematography Workshops and Certifications.** Attend workshops or pursue certifications in cinematography from reputable institutions to strengthen your camera operation and lighting skills.
5. **Pro Tools Certification.** For those interested in sound design and editing, Pro Tools certifications can highlight your proficiency in industry-standard audio software.
6. **Film Production Certificates.** Many universities and film schools offer comprehensive film production certificates covering various aspects of filmmaking.
7. **Digital Marketing Certifications.** As the industry evolves, understanding digital marketing is crucial. Certifications in digital marketing can be valuable for promoting and distributing films effectively.
8. **Project Management Certifications**. Gain certifications in project management, such as PMP (Project Management Professional), to demonstrate your ability to manage film productions efficiently.
9. **Acting Workshops and Certifications.** While not a traditional certification, completing acting workshops and courses can provide insights into the actor's perspective.
10. **Networking Organizations.** Joining and obtaining certifications from industry-specific organizations, like the Producers Guild of America (PGA), can enhance your professional standing.

Always stay current on industry trends and preferences, as the film industry favors a combination of formal education, practical experience, and continual professional growth.

POV

I see myself as an outlier. Most of my peers who finished college eventually went into management positions, and most of my peers on production sets had never been to college. I decided to jump back into the industry with all my higher education and former experience as a production coordinator to take a demotion and become a production assistant—while already having a bachelor's degree in media communications and a master's degree in organizational leadership. It sounds outlandish. No one who ever hired me knew my credentials because I was in an entry-level production position, and there was no need to lead with that. I was there to learn.

One thing you will experience in the industry is new connections to people who will be at the top of their game one day, and you'll forge life-long friendships with people who were in the trenches with you. However, most people are either stepping over someone to get to the top or stepping on someone to keep their spot. For someone like me, who is very empathetic, this was uncomfortable. If people suspect you can replace them, they will often make your life as a production assistant even more miserable. This is the mentality of many people in the industry.

Although I had already obtained higher education and had leadership skills, I put my head down and did the work. I got the coffee. I assisted production managers; I learned what everyone did on set. I helped in other departments so I could find what else interested me. I networked and made connections on every set. This was just a pit stop. If you can hold your head high and put your ego to the side while keeping your head down and doing the work—you might just make it.

During my time as a production assistant, I developed grit and mental fortitude that only grew stronger each year. I am not the same person I was eight years ago. I was humbled to my core and grateful to be where I always wanted to be—behind the scenes on a production set. I imagine it's akin to basic training in the military. You will never be the same once you get through it. You will be demeaned and feel devalued, and be on your feet on and off for multiple 12-hour days. When you've had enough and built a solid resume of work, it will be time for you to level up, pick a track, and be on your way.

By researching and finding out what skills you already have, you can map out your trajectory in the film industry and see where you can pick up additional knowledge on set or through online courses or coaching.

One thing I learned quickly in production is that most technicians have never been to film school. There's even a sort of disdain regarding film school in the industry. It's typically viewed as there are people who learn how to be filmmakers and people who do the work and become filmmakers. Boy, am I glad that I saved thousands and thousands of dollars and didn't take out that additional loan. However, everyone isn't self-taught, and you can't learn on the job if you've never even worked on a set.

However, the fact that most never attended film school or perhaps even college removes one more entry barrier. I'm not against higher learning. There is a place for that in the industry as well.

Specialization is great. It means you can master one area and be known for that skill. The world encourages becoming a specialist. From the moment you arrive at college, you are pushed to choose a discipline. After all, who wants to be a "jack of all trades, master of none"? Again, there are always exceptions to every rule. What if I told you the actual quote is "jack of all trades, master of none, though oftentimes better than a master of one." If you're someone who finds joy in delving into multiple niches, a good communicator with people on all levels and a big-picture thinker, possess project management and leadership skills, have an eye for marketing and a creative vision, then like me, you may be a generalist. A generalist, according to the internet gods, is someone who can specialize in multiple areas, with a balance of knowledge and breadth. They make knowledge connections that specialists cannot make. They are good at synthesis not just analysis. They are very effective at putting their products and services—and the benefits they deliver—in the context of the clients overall goals and strategy. Generalist are adept in multiple areas and turn change into opportunity.

At some point, you will have to turn down jobs that don't promote you to the next level. It's akin to playing a video game. You often get trapped into one role and can't advance upward or sideways.

Most people in the industry will become below-the-line technicians like a camera operator, grip, or gaffer and stay on a specific track. A smaller percentage of people will move into management roles like production coordinator, production manager and above-the-line jobs like producer, director, and showrunner. An even smaller percentage will be executive producers and entertainment executives.

The higher up the chain you go, the more important education, business management, and leadership experience will come into play. Most of these people have never worked a day on set. Just look up the co-CEO of Netflix on LinkedIn. Look at their credentials, and you'll see why having an education can be crucial if you hope to end up at the top of the pyramid.

CHAPTER SEVEN:

LAND A GIG. BE A ROCKSTAR ON SET.

Getting your first job in the film industry is an exciting but difficult venture that involves a combination of passion, skills, and smart networking. You will need to tailor your resume to the standards of the film industry, where you will be highlighting relevant experiences and skills to suit the position you're bidding for. It also involves crafting a strong cover letter that shows that you're the right person for the job.

While making your resume, you must start with a concise, objective statement reflecting your passion for the film industry and your career goals. Also, highlight technical skills such as film editing software proficiency, camera operation, scriptwriting, and any other skills pertinent to the specific job. The resume should also contain a list of any film-related projects, internships, or independent films you've worked on. Include your role, the project's name, and a brief description of your contributions. Emphasize any film-related courses, degrees, or certifications you've obtained. Include relevant coursework and notable projects. Finally, where applicable, provide a link to your online portfolio showcasing your work, including clips, scripts, or any other relevant materials.

Begin your cover letter by expressing your knowledge of the company and its recent projects. Show that you understand its values and mission. The next step is to share a brief personal story that connects your passion for film with the specific role you're applying for. Be authentic and compelling. Demonstrate clearly how your skills and experiences align with the job requirements. Use specific examples to illustrate your capabilities. You are also to convey your genuine enthusiasm for the role and the company. Show that you are not just seeking a job but are excited about contributing to their projects. Finally, end your cover letter with a call to action, expressing your eagerness for an interview and reiterating your enthusiasm for the opportunity.

NETWORKING GROUPS ON FACEBOOK

The purpose of networking groups on Facebook is to create a platform for professionals, job seekers, and employers to connect. These groups aim to facilitate the sharing of job opportunities, career advice, and industry insights within a specific community or industry. Members can network, discuss relevant topics, and stay updated on job openings, fostering a supportive environment for career growth.

However, you will always need to verify the authenticity of any of such groups to avoid scamming. Some groups on Facebook where you can network and are a source for job opportunities are:

1. Film Industry network;
2. Networking for Career Filmmakers;
3. TV and Film production Crew jobs;
4. Film production and jobs;
5. Film & TV Network group Los Angeles;
6. Los Angeles Film Networking;
7. Paid Film/TV Production jobs: Los Angeles area;
8. Actors, Filmmakers, and job postings;
9. NYC Film/TV Gigs (PAID);
10. Media Crew Now;
11. Commercial Filmmakers Network;
12. Videographers Connect;
13. Business for Filmmakers;

14. Film/TV Industry Networking Group;
15. Better Photos, Video, & Editing;
16. Professional Animators;
17. Create CG;
18. The Frugal Filmmaker;
19. Screenwriting;
20. Filmmakers Forum.

You can broaden your search to other social media platforms such as Linkedin, Instagram, Twitter, Thread, etc. Essentially, your dream job may just be one click away from you.

ON-SET ETIQUETTE AND EXPECTATIONS

Now that you have gotten a job, are you prepared for what is expected of you on set? Remember, every job matters, and so does your attitude. Everyone in the film industry has a role that they must play. The filmmaking process proceeds smoothly as long as order is maintained.

When someone disrupts the normal order of things, chaos and misunderstanding follow, which can lead to significant disagreements and even work suspension.

Here are the rules of film set etiquette to familiarize yourself with.

Rule 1: Introductions.

Once you've been chosen as a member of the crew, you must acquaint yourself with everyone on set. Take the time on your first day to introduce yourself to everyone. Don't expect them all to remember your name, but this is a good politeness rule. A proper introduction is the most effective technique to establish contact with your team and ensure the upcoming working process is easy, friendly, and enjoyable.

Rule 2: Each Day Is A New Day.

Whatever happens outside of the set is your personal life and should not affect your professional performance. This is a tried-and-true norm of good manners. You should be committed to performing your finest work every day on set.

When you're working, a hangover, a nasty breakup, or a relative in the hospital shouldn't matter. If you can't keep it all within, requesting sick leave and staying at home for a day is preferable to disrupt the working process.

Rule 3: Mind Your Manners and Keep Your Cool.

Whatever function you play on set, whether director or runner, you must be courteous and accurate in all you say and do with your coworkers. Nobody should know if you're angry or disappointed. Count to ten, use an abacus, and take deep breaths; whatever helps you keep the horses in check will do. On set, be cautious and thoughtful.

Rule 4: Respect The Silence.

You're aware that once the director shouts, "Action!" there can be no sound on set except for the actors executing their jobs. And you must keep this rule in mind! Yes, smartphones are a major and crucial part of many people's toolkits on set. However, you must not allow the unexpected sound to disrupt the scene. Turn off the cell phone's volume and ensure that even the vibration is not audible to anyone around you.

Aside from the phone, keep a watch on your overall noise level. The less there is, the better. Most celebrities dislike loud employees; thus, you shouldn't get fixed into this category.

Rule 5: Know Your Role.

Every worker on a film set is a key organ in a single organism. You must realize that no matter what you do, you are significant, and your job is significant. So, there's no need to try to tell a director how to block a scene or a director of photography how to accent a character's cheek. Such remarks annoy the recipients and disrupt the crew's common understanding.

You know what your role is, so carry it out. If everyone adheres to the pattern, the film will be completed in no time! In short, mind your business.

Rule 6: Trust Your Team.

Industry experts emphasize the need to rely on one another during production because the project's completion depends on all participants. Of course, there can be an issue of trust in the initial team selection, but after you've chosen these individuals, trust them. Proceed based on the professionalism and competence of the personnel you've chosen.

Rule 7: Don't Move Anything Over Which You Have No Authority.

Every single object on set has a place. Don't touch anything if you don't know where it belongs! You're likely to relocate set props and then make a terrible mistake that will tarnish the film's reputation. Stay in your department and only work on items you are familiar with. If something appears in your way, it does not necessarily imply it is.

Rule 8: Pay Close Attention.

It is part of the job description of a film crew to pay attention to everything that happens around them. You must not only listen to what the director says, but also to the rest of your staff. For example, before plugging in your phone charger, ensure it won't damage the lighting on stage. As an assistant, you must understand what belongs where and who likes what. Don't forget about the changes in the first and last lists, as well as the good and poor days. This knowledge is critical to your career!

Rule 9: Be Careful What You Wear.

Even though the film set is not a bank with strict dress code regulations, there are still guidelines that must be followed. Nobody is talking about specific prohibitions, but it's always a good idea to keep your appearance in mind. Try to keep as comfortable as possible on set because running in heels or changing the light in a suit is not a good idea!

Aside from that, watch out for colors. Bright shirts, for example, (such as yellow, white, and even light grays) can alter the lighting of a scene by adding unwanted color tones.

Rule 10: Be Understanding.

According to a Dolly Grip, "I understand" is a universal response on set. "I understand." is the best answer to any question or directive. Aside from the "I understand" response, it's always helpful to repeat the question in your response because it shows the person who asked you that you received the message. For example: "Can you grab a hot brick from the cart when you get a chance? "... "copy." ... "copy, what?!" The responder is expected to say, "copy, I can grab a hot brick from the cart." This tactic is especially important when you use a walkie-talkie for communication on set.

Rule 11: Be a Ninja.

Everyone on set admires ninjas because they are always at the correct place at the right time, do their job flawlessly, and stay silent and undetected when necessary. Being quiet on set entails not only not talking when the camera is rolling but also shutting off your cell phone and refraining from asking irrelevant questions.

Rule 12: Do Not Disappear.

Never leave the set without informing anyone! Regardless of your position in the filmmaking process, if you're present, you're crucial. Sometimes, the entire filming process is halted because a makeup artist failed to notify someone that they were leaving early or a cleaner failed to remove the garbage can.

Remember that leaving your office is generally considered bad manners in any employment. And keep in mind that you're working with artists whose moods can be ruined in an instant. To minimize issues, always notify someone near you while taking a break or using the restroom.

Rule 13: Learn The Language.

Proper language onset is not just an element of film set etiquette but also a necessary skill for anyone involved in the filmmaking process. Gary Collins, CEO of Red Rock Entertainment, believes this is the most crucial guideline on set. You won't be able to understand what your director says unless you learn the language.

Make sure you understand the terminology used throughout the film business as well as the vocabulary unique to your set. To give you a head start, we've included some of the most common set lingo in the glossary chapter that will make you look like a pro on your first production gig.

Rule 14: Learn The Rules on Set.

Some studios, for example, do not begin production until the lead actor has a cup of coffee or a director goes around the set for a quick check. These are minor details that go unnoticed but have a significant impact on the entire filmmaking process. Keep an eye out for "rituals" and inquire around if you don't see any. However, remember to ask wisely.

Regardless of how involved you are in the filmmaking process, how much you enjoy your job, and how stringent the rules are on your specific set, you must remember that your life is far more valuable than any job or film made in history!

You must contact someone immediately if you feel unsafe or alert at all times. Yes, you may be ridiculed, but stick to your guts. You never know when your determination and inner strength will save your own or a colleague's life.

Rule 14: Don't Get Star Struck.

You should not get starstruck by celebrities, ask for autographs, or take pictures of them.

BUILDING RELATIONSHIPS AND GAINING EXPERIENCE — A WAY TO DISCOVER YOUR NICHE

Relationships are the bedrock of the film industry. Thus, every aspiring filmmaker who desires to succeed must build quality relationships in the industry. Here are some guidelines on how to do so.

1. **Be Proactive and Prepare**

    Seeking opportunities to meet and interact with people who share your passion and vision is one of the first steps toward developing long-lasting relationships in the film industry. Film festivals, workshops, screenings, online forums, and social media groups are all possibilities. However, you should not simply turn up and hope for the best. Conduct preliminary research to determine who you want to speak with, what you want to learn from them, and what you can offer them. Prepare a clear and succinct pitch to introduce yourself and your business, as well as relevant and engaging questions.

2. **Be Respectful and Supportive**

    Treat everyone you meet with dignity and professionalism, regardless of their function or rank. Keep in mind that the film industry is a small and linked world, and you never know who your next collaborator, employer, or mentor may be. As a result, be kind, polite, and attentive to everyone with whom you engage, and refrain from gossiping, criticizing, or complaining. Instead, express gratitude, offer praises, and assist wherever possible. Attending events, sharing your work, and contributing productively to conversations are all ways to show your support for your fellow filmmakers.

3. **Be Consistent and Genuine**

    Finally, developing long-term connections in the film industry necessitates consistent and genuine communication. Don't only network when you need something or want to promote something. Maintain regular contact with your contacts and express genuine interest in their ideas, challenges, and accomplishments. Send them updates, stories, invitations, or referrals that they may find interesting or relevant. Be open, honest, and real about your objectives, expectations, and obstacles. Make no false promises or try to be someone you are not. Allow your individuality and passion to shine through.

By following these tips, you can build lasting relationships in the film industry that will not only help you advance your career but also enrich your personal and professional life.

GAINING EXPERIENCE IN THE FILM INDUSTRY

Gaining experiences is a crucial component of continuous learning and growth. Experiences, whether positive or challenging, provide valuable lessons, shape perspectives, and contribute to developing skills and resilience. Embracing diverse experiences helps individuals broaden their horizons, adapt to change, and enhance their problem-solving abilities. These are some ways in which one can gain relevant experience:

1. Discover your Niche

Film production is a broad term that includes a variety of roles and responsibilities. Are you interested in becoming a director, producer, cinematographer, editor, sound designer, or something else? Each role comes with its own set of challenges, responsibilities, and expectations. You should investigate the various components of film production to choose what best suits your interests, strengths, and ambitions.

2. Learn the basic concepts

Once you've determined your specialty, you need to study the fundamentals of film production. This entails being acquainted with the equipment, software, terminology, and practices pertinent to your chosen profession. Online classes, books, podcasts, blogs, and YouTube videos are good places to start. You can also attend workshops, seminars, or short courses that provide on-the-job training and feedback. Learning the fundamentals will assist you in developing your confidence, portfolio, and credibility.

3. Make your own projects

Creating your own projects is one of the finest methods to obtain film-producing abilities without prior experience. Making a film does not require a large budget, a high-end camera, or a professional team. You may shoot and edit a short film, a documentary, a music video, or a web series with your smartphone, laptop, and friends. You can also share your work on internet platforms like Vimeo, YouTube, or TikTok and receive comments from other filmmakers and viewers. Making your own projects will allow you to hone your abilities, demonstrate your talent, and express your creativity.

4. Networking with other filmmakers

Filmmaking is a community, and your network of production people are the ones who keep you working. You can connect with others who share your interests and aspirations by joining online communities such as Facebook groups, Reddit forums, or LinkedIn groups. You can also attend local events such as film festivals, screenings, or meetups to meet and interact with industry professionals. Networking with other filmmakers will allow you to learn from their mistakes, locate mentors, and uncover new opportunities.

5. Volunteering

A great way to gain film production experience without prior experience is to volunteer or intern for film projects. You can look for opportunities on websites, such as Mandy, Production HUB, or Film Local, where you can find listings for various film jobs and gigs. You can also reach out to local filmmakers, production companies, or organizations looking for help with their projects. Volunteering or interning for film projects will help you gain valuable exposure, insight, and contacts.

Building relationships and accumulating experiences, in essence, constitute a dynamic basis for a rich and rewarding life. The relationships we form with others, and the lessons we gain from our experiences all contribute to our overall personal and professional growth, making us more resilient, adaptive, and compassionate.

WORKING ON FILM SETS

Going behind the scenes of a film is an immersive trip into the core of storytelling and creativity. This dynamic atmosphere, in which vision is brought to life via the lens, necessitates a delicate mix of teamwork, networking, and skillful relationship management. Emerging filmmakers face the complexities of team relationships, resource optimization, and the art of networking on set in this arena. This chapter illustrates the road for individuals wishing to enter the enthralling world of film production, providing insights into the collaborative spirit, professional ties, and the interplay between personal and professional relationships that constitute the foundation of a successful cinematic enterprise.

COLLABORATING WITH FELLOW UPCOMING FILMMAKERS ON INDIE FILM PROJECTS

Independent movies, often referred to as indie films, are films that are produced outside the major film studio system. Unlike mainstream studio productions, independent movies are typically financed, produced, and distributed by independent filmmakers, production companies, or small studios. These films are known for their artistic and creative expression, often exploring unconventional themes and storytelling approaches.

Notable examples of independent films include *Clerks* by Kevin Smith, *Little Miss Sunshine* by Jonathan Dayton and Valerie Faris, and the Oscar award-winning film *Moonlight* by Barry Jenkins. Independent cinema is crucial in providing diverse voices and perspectives in the film industry, offering an alternative to mainstream commercial filmmaking.

Collaborating with a fellow upcoming filmmaker in indie filmmaking can offer a range of benefits and opportunities. Here are several compelling reasons to consider collaboration with your peers:

1. **Shared Vision and Passion.** Collaborating with someone who shares your passion for filmmaking ensures a common

creative vision. This shared enthusiasm can lead to a more dedicated and inspired collaboration.

2. **Combined Skills and Expertise.** Each filmmaker brings a unique set of skills and expertise to the table. By collaborating, you can leverage each other's strengths, potentially enhancing the overall quality of the project.

3. **Resource Maximization.** Indie filmmaking often involves working with limited resources. Collaborating allows you to pool resources, share equipment, and potentially access a broader network of contacts, which can be crucial for overcoming budget constraints.

4. **Learning and Growth.** Collaborating with another filmmaker provides an opportunity for mutual learning and growth. You can exchange ideas, learn new techniques, and broaden your understanding of different aspects of filmmaking.

5. **Problem-Solving Dynamics.** Filmmaking comes with its share of challenges and problem-solving moments. Working with a collaborator can provide diverse perspectives, enhancing your ability to navigate and overcome obstacles creatively.

6. **Increased Productivity.** With a well-coordinated team, tasks can be distributed more efficiently, leading to increased productivity. This can be particularly valuable when facing tight deadlines or working on multiple aspects of a project simultaneously.

7. **Networking Opportunities.** Collaborating with another filmmaker introduces you to their network of contacts and collaborators. This expanded network can open doors to new opportunities, including potential funding, distribution, or future projects.

8. **Emotional Support.** The filmmaking process can be demanding, both creatively and emotionally. Having a collaborator provides emotional support and someone to share the highs and lows of the filmmaking journey.

9. **Division of Responsibilities.** By collaborating, you can divide responsibilities based on each filmmaker's strengths

and interests. This can lead to a more streamlined workflow and ensure that each aspect of the project receives the attention it deserves.

10. **Increased Motivation.** Filmmaking is often a long and challenging process. Having a collaborator can provide motivation and encouragement, helping both filmmakers stay committed to the project.

In indie filmmaking, where creativity often thrives on collaboration and resourcefulness, partnering with a fellow filmmaker can amplify the potential for success and create a richer, more fulfilling filmmaking experience.

NETWORKING ON SET

Networking on a film set is an important part of developing contacts and opportunities in the film business. Here are some crucial networking strategies for on-set success:

1. **Professionalism and Manners.** Be prompt, prepared, and appreciative of everyone's position on set to demonstrate professionalism. Respect fellow crew members and follow set decorum, such as avoiding disturbing scenes.

2. **Always Introduce Yourself.** Introduce yourself to people on set, particularly those you haven't worked with previously. A welcoming and approachable personality may generate a good first impression.

3. **Learn Roles and Names**. Take note of the names and roles of the persons you meet. Addressing coworkers by name and recognizing their accomplishments builds a sense of community.

4. **Participate in Conversations.** During downtime or breaks, strike up a discussion. Discussing the project, exchanging experiences, or expressing interest in the work of others might result in important connections.

5. **Ask Questions.** Be truly interested in other people's work. Inquiring about their jobs, experiences, and difficulties demonstrates interest while also opening the door for more discussion.

6. **Take Part in Group Activities.** Participate heartily in any group activities or team-building exercises taking place on set. This may create informal environments for networking and connection development.

7. **Exchange Contact Information.** Exchange contact information, including social media accounts, with other crew members. This makes it easy to remain in touch and track each other's progress outside the present project.

8. **Participate in Crew Events.** Attend any social parties or gatherings planned for actors and crew. These gatherings provide a comfortable setting for networking and getting to know individuals outside the workplace.

9. **Be Receptive to Collaboration.** Express your readiness to work on future initiatives with others. Making others aware of your willingness to collaborate develops a feeling of community and can lead to collaboration possibilities.

10. **Provide Help and Support.** Be willing to assist people on set, whether with duties, giving expertise, or providing support. Acts of kindness help to create a healthy work environment and can build professional ties.

11. **Demonstrate Your Skills.** Display your abilities and knowledge when appropriate. Whether it's describing a specific approach or presenting your portfolio, it can make you a desirable contact for future tasks.

12. **Reach Out After the Project.** After the project is completed, follow up with the folks you've met. Express thanks for the partnership and indicate a desire to remain in touch for potential future initiatives.

Effective networking on set is about developing a supportive community within the film business as well as boosting one's profession. You contribute to a collaborative and healthy film community by making true relationships and actively interacting with colleagues.

MANAGING PERSONAL AND PROFESSIONAL RELATIONSHIPS

Managing private and personal relationships on a movie set requires a delicate balance to ensure a professional environment. Here are some tips:

1. **Set Clear Boundaries.** Establish clear boundaries between personal and professional life. Clearly define when you're "on set" and in your personal space.
2. **Professionalism**. Maintain a high level of professionalism during work hours. Treat your partner or friend on set as you would any other colleague.
3. **Separate Roles.** If you work in different capacities (e.g., actor and director), keep those roles distinct while on set. Focus on the job at hand and avoid personal conflicts affecting your professional work.
4. **Open Communication.** Before starting the project, discuss expectations and potential challenges with your partner or friend. Open communication can prevent misunderstandings and conflicts.
5. **Respect Others.** Be mindful of how your personal relationship may impact others on set. Avoid displaying excessive affection or engaging in private discussions that could make others uncomfortable.
6. **Problem Resolution**. If conflicts arise, address them promptly and professionally. Seek solutions that maintain the harmony of the working environment.
7. **Maintain Professionalism with Crew**. Ensure your personal relationship doesn't lead to favoritism or bias. Treat everyone on set with fairness and respect.
8. **Time Management.** Balance your time effectively between personal and professional commitments. Avoid neglecting work responsibilities or letting personal matters interfere with the project.

Remember, the key is to prioritize the project's success and the entire team's well-being while still nurturing your personal relationships.

P⦿V

My first production gig was at the world-renowned Tribeca International Film Festival. This is an annual festival that takes place in New York City and is attended by the press, celebrities, and filmmakers from around the world. The legendary Robert DeNiro and Jane Rosenthal co-founded the film festival. I landed my first gig in event production and was adjacent to world premiere films, legendary filmmakers, new filmmakers, and movie fans who descended onto the scene in New York City's Tribeca neighborhood. I was stationed at the SVA theater as a screening manager. I wasn't on a film or TV production set, but this was the next best thing.

Working behind the scenes in entertainment isn't limited to working on a TV or film production. It includes working film festivals, red carpets for awards shows, radio shows, podcasts, and concerts. These are all types of entertainment productions that are great for networking and help build your portfolio with various job experiences. People like us run everything in entertainment for human consumption behind the scenes.

I nabbed my first production gig at Tribeca pretty easily. It's all in the timing. It also looks good on your production resume if you got your feet wet at the country's most significant film festival. You don't have to go straight for Tribeca like I did. I approached several. It also helped that I had a brother who lived in nearby New Jersey who let me crash at his home for two weeks and a family friend who let me crash with him in the Bronx. Either try to locate a festival in your hometown, a neighboring city or state, where you can secure free room and board, and the pay to work at a festival may be worth it. They don't pay a ton, but the networking and experience are invaluable.

My strategy involved making a spreadsheet of every film festival on the East Coast and documenting the start date of each festival, followed by a contact number that I would find for "job opportunities," which is usually located at the bottom of any festival website. They are seasonal jobs, so they won't be posted until a few months from the festival date.

I made it a habit to use my spreadsheet to determine when would be the best time to check the website's job postings, which was usually 3-4 months out from the festival start date. Usually, festivals will start posting all sorts of jobs and volunteer jobs, from the box office and registration to theater screening management, venue management, and many more. I went after the paid jobs, but if you want to increase your likelihood of selection, you can go for the volunteer jobs, and then for the next festival, you'll have at least one festival job on your resume. Make sure to keep references and contacts after each gig. Let the person who brought you in know that you appreciate it and to call you if they require more assistance in the future.

Working at a film festival and setting up red carpets and seating for VIPs is inspiring. Sitting amongst legendary filmmakers and producers who, at some point, took a chance to follow their dreams will make you feel like you are on the right path.

One of my fondest experiences was working at the Tribeca Film Festival at SVA, where we screened the animated short film called *Dear Basketball,* written and narrated by Kobe Bryant. It was a moving account of the moment he fell in love with basketball through the moment he retired. Seeing in animated form what basketball meant to him through his own narration hit me deeply and brought me to tears. I remember seating Kobe and his wife Vanessa and sitting in the aisle across from them during the screening. The entire audience cheered and applauded as the credits rolled and the lights slowly came up. I looked over and could see the huge smile across his face as he waved. That animated short film went on to win an Oscar.

To land your first few gigs, you have to be willing to do the job that no one wants to do. One of those jobs for me was for the presidential inauguration. I can't tell you how many things were going through my head. At that moment, I decided to separate my politics to gain an opportunity. It was the right move. Because it was controversial, I was able to land the gig easily as several people, including talent, began to pull out at the last minute. On that set, I met half a dozen people of diverse backgrounds and ethnicities whom I networked with and who would later refer me to more and more gigs. It was the gig that kept on giving.

One thing I learned early on is the importance of preparedness, and that includes creating an authentic version of yourself that is ready to jump in and get the job done. When you are hired for a production, it can be a very intimidating experience. You are surrounded by hustling and bustling people at the top of their field. You don't know if you need to stand still aimlessly or jump in and try to help.

One of the first things I was flagged on during one of my first production gigs was when the producer offered to give me a piece of advice. He said always to look busy—even if it means clearing the trash cans every 20 minutes. It sounds silly, but when technicians are at work, they are eating on the go and leaving trash behind, and there's not really a person assigned to clear the trash. You have now owned that job and become a useful body. To be unnoticed in a good way is the best way to stand out. When you are constantly moving, you don't attract attention. A surefire way to stand out, and not for good reason, is by sitting down or wandering.

Production is a fast-paced environment and is always changing. Be ready and make yourself available. There was a political docuseries I worked with for a couple of seasons. I never knew when they would be coming into town. Still, they relied on me for many time-sensitive jobs, like picking up political hosts from the airport and driving to different states to deliver footage, and even pick up talent's personal vehicles. You have to earn that kind of trust. The show was so run-and-gun they would pay me a day rate just to be on standby at home. The jobs will get better with experience, I promise. At that time, the rate for an entry position as a production assistant was a day rate of $200.

CHAPTER EIGHT:
GET YOUR WORK NOTICED

Making your work stand out in the film industry is a big challenge. Whether you're a filmmaker, writer, or part of film production, getting noticed is crucial for your career. This guide will explore practical ways to gain attention, like using film festivals, building industry relationships, and social media. Following these strategies can boost your work, expand your network, and make a mark in the competitive film industry.

THE ROLE OF FILM FESTIVALS IN GETTING YOUR WORK NOTICED

Film festivals play a pivotal role in showcasing the work of upcoming filmmakers for several key reasons:

1. **Exposure to Industry Professionals**. Film festivals attract producers, distributors, and industry insiders. By participating, upcoming filmmakers can get their work in front of professionals who can offer deals, collaborations, or further opportunities.

2. **Audience Recognition**. Festivals provide a platform for filmmakers to connect directly with audiences. Positive responses and feedback from viewers can generate buzz and enhance a filmmaker's reputation, potentially leading to more opportunities.

3. **Validation and Credibility**. Selection for prestigious film festivals serves as a form of validation for an upcoming filmmaker's work. Being part of a reputable festival enhances credibility and may attract attention from critics, studios, and other filmmakers.

4. **Networking Opportunities**. Film festivals offer a unique environment for networking. Filmmakers can interact with peers, industry professionals, and potential collaborators. Building relationships at festivals can open doors to future projects and collaborations.
5. **International Reach**. Many film festivals attract a diverse, international audience. This exposure can be especially valuable for upcoming filmmakers seeking recognition beyond their local or national borders, potentially leading to global distribution opportunities.
6. **Learning and Inspiration**. Attending film festivals allows filmmakers to watch a diverse range of films, gaining insights into different storytelling techniques, styles, and trends. This exposure can serve as a source of inspiration and contribute to the growth and development of their own craft.
7. **Awards and Recognition**. Winning or even being nominated for awards at film festivals can significantly boost a filmmaker's profile. Awards can act as a stamp of approval and attract attention from both the industry and the general public.

In summary, film festivals offer a crucial platform for upcoming filmmakers to showcase their work, gain recognition, connect with industry professionals, and propel their careers to new heights.

SELECTING THE RIGHT FILM FESTIVAL FOR YOUR CONTENT

Choosing the right film festivals for your content is a crucial step in gaining exposure and maximizing the impact of your work. Here are key considerations to help you make informed decisions:

1. **Genre Alignment**. Identify festivals that align with the genre and style of your content. Some festivals specialize in specific genres, ensuring your work reaches an audience genuinely interested in your type of film.

2. **Audience Demographics.** Consider the demographics of the festival's audience. Choose festivals where your target audience is likely to be present, increasing the chances of your work resonating with viewers who appreciate your content.
3. **Festival Prestige.** Balance your submissions between renowned, high-profile festivals and smaller, niche ones. Being selected for prestigious festivals adds credibility to your work, while smaller festivals may provide unique opportunities and a platform for recognition.
4. **Submission Criteria.** Review submission criteria, including eligibility, deadlines, and any specific requirements. Ensure your content complies with these guidelines to maximize your chances of being considered.
5. **Networking Opportunities.** Research festivals that offer strong networking opportunities. Festivals with industry events, panels, and Q&A sessions provide valuable chances to connect with professionals, potentially opening doors for future collaborations.
6. **Geographic Reach.** Consider the geographic reach of the festival. Depending on your goals, you may opt for local, national, or international festivals. This choice can impact the diversity of your audience and the potential for global exposure.
7. **Budget Considerations.** Evaluate the cost of submissions and attendance. While prestigious festivals may have higher fees, the exposure can be worth the investment. Factor in travel and accommodation expenses if you plan to attend in person.
8. **Past Success Stories.** Look into the history of the festival and its impact on filmmakers. Festivals that have helped launch the careers of emerging talents might be favorable choices for your work.

By carefully assessing these factors, you can tailor your submissions to festivals that align with your content, goals, and the audience you aim to reach, increasing the likelihood of your work being noticed and appreciated.

CRAFTING COMPELLING SUBMISSION

Creating compelling submissions for film festivals is essential to grab the attention of selection committees. Here are some tips and strategies:

1. **Follow Guidelines**. Read and follow the submission guidelines carefully. Ensure that your submission meets all the specified requirements regarding format, duration, and any additional materials.

2. **Highlight Unique Elements**. Clearly communicate what makes your film stand out. Whether it's a unique story, innovative technique, or powerful performance, emphasize these distinctive aspects in your submission.

3. **Engaging Synopsis.** Write a concise and engaging synopsis. Clearly convey your film's central theme, characters, and emotional impact. Make it compelling to capture the reviewers' interest from the start.

4. **Quality Trailer or Clip.** Include a well-edited trailer or a captivating clip from your film. This provides a visual preview of your work and helps reviewers understand its visual and storytelling qualities.

5. **Director's Statement**. Write a brief director's statement to provide insight into your creative process and intentions. Share what inspired the project and any challenges overcome during production.

6. **Professional Presentation**. Ensure that your submission is professionally presented. High-quality visuals, sound, and overall production value in your submission materials reflect positively on your work.

7. **Previous Successes**. If applicable, mention any awards, recognitions, or screenings your film has received. Highlighting previous successes can build confidence in the quality of your work.

8. **Targeted Cover Letter.** Write a brief, targeted cover letter expressing your enthusiasm for the specific festival. Personalize it by mentioning why you believe your film aligns with the festival's values or themes.

9. **Early Submission**. Submit your entry before the deadline, if possible. Early submissions may receive more attention, and they demonstrate your commitment to the festival.
10. **Professional Contact Information**. Provide clear and professional contact information. Ensure that festival organizers can easily reach you if they have questions or need further information.

By incorporating these tips into your submission strategy, you enhance the chances of making a lasting impression on festival selection committees and increasing the visibility of your work in the competitive festival circuit.

WORKING AT FILM FESTIVALS

Working at film festivals can offer valuable experiences and insights into the industry. Here's how you can make the most of your involvement:

1. **Volunteer Opportunities**. Seek volunteer positions at film festivals. This provides hands-on experience, access to industry professionals, and a chance to contribute to the event's success.
2. **Networking**. Actively engage with filmmakers, industry insiders, and fellow volunteers. Networking at festivals can lead to connections that may open doors for future collaborations or opportunities.
3. **Learn the Behind-the-Scenes**. Gain a deeper understanding of festival operations by working in various roles. This can include ticketing, event coordination, or assisting with screenings. Learning the logistical aspects enhances your overall industry knowledge.
4. **Attend Industry Events.** Take advantage of industry-specific events within the festival, such as panel discussions, workshops, and Q&A sessions. These opportunities allow you to learn from professionals and stay updated on industry trends.
5. **Build Relationships With Organizers**. Establish connections with festival organizers and staff. Express your interest

in the industry and seek advice. Building relationships with those behind the scenes can provide valuable insights and potential future opportunities.

6. **Promote Your Skills.** If relevant, showcase your own skills or projects. This could include volunteering to assist with promotional materials, social media management, or contributing to festival-related content.

7. **Stay Informed**. Stay informed about the films being showcased. Attend screenings and familiarize yourself with different genres and styles. This knowledge can be beneficial in future endeavors within the film industry.

8. **Be Adaptable.** Film festivals can be fast-paced and dynamic. Be adaptable to different tasks and responsibilities, showcasing your ability to handle diverse challenges in the industry.

9. **Seek Feedback**. If possible, seek feedback on your work or contributions. Constructive feedback from experienced professionals can provide valuable insights into areas for improvement and growth.

10. **Document Your Experience**. Keep a record of your experiences, tasks, and the people you meet. This documentation can serve as a reference for future opportunities, job applications, or networking endeavors.

Working at film festivals not only offers a unique perspective on the industry but also provides a platform to connect with like-minded individuals. Embrace the learning opportunities, contribute enthusiastically, and use the experience to further your career in the dynamic world of film.

PROMOTING YOUR WORK ON SOCIAL MEDIA

For film promotions on social media, leverage platforms like Instagram, Twitter, and Facebook. Share engaging behind-the-scenes content, teasers, and exclusive sneak peeks. Collaborate with influencers and use relevant hashtags. Host contests and live Q&A sessions to build anticipation leading to the release. Encourage audience participation and feedback.

POV

As of the writing of this publication, Tribeca Film Festival announced that they are launching their own distribution for films on their festival roster that will be distributed to streaming platforms. This will open the door for many more indie filmmakers to achieve success. I happen to know a woman who specializes in film festival strategy and can help filmmakers create a festival strategy for independent films. If you've never been on the film festival circuit, this is a crucial step so that you don't make a misstep and miss your window of opportunity.

It is one thing to make a film—it is another thing to find success after you make that film. You don't want to squander all your time, energy, and resources and end up with a film project you can't sell and collects dust on a shelf. So, when building out your film budget with your producer, be sure to factor in costs for a marketing and film festival strategy.

One of the biggest things new filmmakers overlook is how they will market their project after spending their entire budget on producing the film. I had the opportunity to produce an indie film, and we had a nice festival run. The goal wasn't to sell the film but to bring awareness, and so it achieved its goal. Be clear about what your goal is when you produce your film project.

It's also worth mentioning a very important piece many new filmmakers overlook: who owns the film's IP (intellectual property). This often isn't discussed until it's time to negotiate deal terms to sell the film. Not having a proper chain of ownership can end up being a costly endeavor with attorneys to unravel and could cost you the distribution deal or cause its delay.

If you can, you should hire a proper entertainment attorney with experience negotiating deal terms or having that discussion up front with your filmmaking team about the ownership of the film's IP. This can be as simple as writing down on a piece of paper or typing out an agreement that all parties sign off on. Ensure you have the proper licensing and permits before filming because that can also derail your distribution deal. If a friend produced a music track for your film and you didn't have it expressly stated who owns it, this can come back to haunt you when you want to sell or distribute the film.

The last vital piece of information I can give you pertains to human behavior and how it factors into getting your work noticed outside of the steps listed in this chapter. When we are just getting our feet wet, we often do things for free and without recognition of our work. It's akin to paying your dues like you would as a production assistant.

Like myself, you will eventually encounter people who will indirectly or directly not attribute your creative contribution in the earliest stages of your career. Getting credit for your ideas is vital, but so is getting your foot in the door to get the opportunity to display your work. This has happened to me many times on my journey, and I can't begin to describe the anguish of not being acknowledged for your creative input. It feels like an implosion inside you that no one else can see. You watch other people get the praise. Your eyes well up with tears that never fall, and you take the win silently.

Let me share two of those stories—one occurred at the beginning of my journey, and the other occurred much later after establishing my professional boundaries. The key is knowing when to concede and when to speak up.

I recall the first time I was given the reigns to produce a professional video project with a budget. I put my heart and soul into producing this project. I hired the film crew, scouted the locations, did the interviews, and traveled to other cities. I sat for hours in post-production, editing in real-time alongside the editor and selecting the music track that perfectly captured an emotional story that brought tears to our eyes in the editing bay. It was the first time I realized I was a real storyteller—that I could move through all aspects of a project from development to post-production, woven into a coherent and colorful tapestry.

I wowed the room of internal stakeholders, as indicated by the applause and feedback. When the lights came up, the attention went straight to the senior producer who had given me the reigns. I had never experienced this before, and all I could think of was quitting on the spot. This next part is why it is important to have mentors in your life—you can blow up your path before you even get started.

I reached out to cousin P, who had achieved global success in music and film as a mega-producer by this time. After picking myself up off the floor, I sent him a message that read like one big run-on sentence of emotions, and I told him that someone was given credit for my work and I wanted to quit. I asked him, "Is this what happened to you when you produced your first hit song?"

His response wasn't what I expected and didn't validate my experience. He said, "Credit isn't taken. It's given, and it may not be your season yet to be acknowledged."

He explained to me that his contribution to the song was not about getting acknowledged but about gaining access to tools to hone his skills while having proximity to another music legend from his town. That alone was a huge opportunity. He proceeded to ask me if I would have been able to produce the video on my own and have access to a budget had I not been given the opportunity. My answer was an obvious "no." I conceded and returned to work. I asked for more projects to hone my skills until it was time for me to move on with several produced projects added to my online portfolio.

At some point, you have to know when conceding is not an option. Later in my journey, after several years of contributing and paying my dues, I was hired to cast hundreds of background actors for a film project. The work a few others and I had done to cast those actors was nothing short of a miracle. We had been asked to source background actors from diverse communities between two cities. It took a lot of grassroots movement and partnerships with community leaders and organizations. There was talk of bringing busloads of people up North from Georgia to fill in the gaps, and producers even considered canceling the largest background scenes that were monumental to the film. I had put all my time, energy, and effort into recruiting and connecting with people across the city and connecting community leaders with production for locations, casting, and props. I was proud of the work I had done as a part of the background casting team.

Almost two years later and multiple delays due to the pandemic, the film was finally making its world premiere at one of the most prominent film festivals in the country, the Toronto International Film Festival. Sure enough, as the credits rolled up the screen, I noticed that a few others and I had been omitted from the film's credits. I watched the background casting director gleefully post screenshots of the film credits of her name and a few others. This was when I decided I had paid enough dues, and I wouldn't concede.

Before that movie would be released in theaters across the country, I had decided that my name being omitted was not an option. I reached out to the production company's executive producer and laid out to them what appeared to be a gross admission. I didn't receive a response. So I took it a step further. I contacted the behemoth media company directly and laid out my case again to its global production manager.

Within 48 hours, I received a response. He genuinely thanked me for my contributions to the film and apologized for the omission. He said it would be corrected in post-production before the film's theatrical release. I went on to provide him with the names of several others who worked alongside me, which had also been omitted. Still, I wondered if they would actually follow through. They did.

Know when it's your season to learn and when it's your season to be acknowledged. Understand when you are given an opportunity for growth and when you need to be your own best advocate.

CHAPTER NINE:

UNION VS NON-UNION: TO JOIN OR NOT TO JOIN?

UNION ROLES VS NON-UNION ROLES

Unions play a significant role in the American film industry, representing various professionals involved in producing films, television shows, and other forms of visual media. These unions negotiate on behalf of their members to secure fair wages, working conditions, and benefits. Here are some key unions in the American film industry:

1. **Screen Actors Guild – American Federation of Television and Radio Artists (SAG-AFTRA).** SAG-AFTRA is a merger of two unions: the Screen Actors Guild (SAG) and the American Federation of Television and Radio Artists (AFTRA). It represents actors, announcers, broadcast journalists, and other media professionals. The Screen Actors Guild (SAG) is a labor union that represents actors in the entertainment industry in the United States. It was originally established in 1933 as the Screen Actors Guild of America (SAGA). It later merged with the American Federation of Television and Radio Artists (AFTRA) in 2012 to form SAG-AFTRA.

To become a member, actors must have a certain level of professional experience and meet specific eligibility criteria. One of the primary functions of SAG is to negotiate and enforce collective bargaining agreements (CBAs) on behalf of its members. These agreements set the terms and conditions of employment for actors, including issues such as wages, working hours, and benefits.

SAG establishes industry standards for contracts, ensuring that actors receive fair compensation and working conditions. These standards cover various aspects of the entertainment industry, from film and television to new media platforms.

Also, SAG works to protect the rights of its members by advocating for fair treatment, preventing exploitation, and addressing issues such as workplace harassment. SAG equally provides health and pension benefits to its members. These benefits help support actors in their careers and provide financial security, especially during periods of unemployment.

SAG organizes the annual Screen Actors Guild Awards, which recognize outstanding performances in film and television. The members of the guild vote on the awards.

The Screen Actors Guild Foundation, now part of the SAG-AFTRA Foundation, is a charitable organization affiliated with SAG. It provides educational programs, scholarships, and emergency assistance to actors.

Overall, the Screen Actors Guild plays a crucial role in advocating for the rights and interests of actors in the dynamic and competitive entertainment industry.

2. **Directors Guild of America (DGA):** The Directors Guild of America (DGA) is a professional organization representing directors, assistant directors, unit production managers, and stage managers in the film, television, and new media industries in the United States.

    The DGA was founded in 1936 to address issues related to working conditions, wages, and the creative rights of directors. Over the years, it has become a powerful and influential organization in the entertainment industry.

    Directors, assistant directors, unit production managers, and stage managers working in film, television, commercials, and new media can become members of the DGA. The membership process typically involves meeting certain professional qualifications and obtaining work credits within the industry.

One of the primary functions of the DGA is to negotiate collective bargaining agreements (CBAs) with producers and studios on behalf of its members. These agreements set industry standards for wages, working conditions, and other terms of employment. Also, the DGA monitors and enforces the terms of its collective bargaining agreements.

It ensures that its members receive fair compensation, proper working conditions, and credited for their work.

The DGA advocates for the creative rights of directors, aiming to ensure that directors have artistic control over their projects. This includes issues related to the final cut, the director's vision, and protection against interference from studios or producers.

The DGA provides training and educational programs to its members to enhance their skills and knowledge. This includes workshops, seminars, and other resources to help members stay current with industry trends and technologies.

Furthermore, The DGA hosts the annual Directors Guild of America Awards, which honor outstanding directorial achievement in various categories, including film and television. The awards are highly regarded in the industry and often serve as indicators of success during the awards season. It also has various committees that focus on specific aspects of the industry, such as diversity and inclusion, safety, and new media. These committees work to address emerging issues and advocate for the interests of DGA members.

The Directors Guild of America is crucial in ensuring the well-being and professional development of directors and related professionals in the entertainment industry. Through its collective bargaining efforts, advocacy for creative rights, and commitment to education, the DGA contributes to the overall health and success of the filmmaking and television industry in the United States.

3. **Producers Guild of America (PGA):** The Producers Guild of America (PGA) is a professional trade organization that represents film, television, and new media producers in the entertainment industry.

The Producers Guild of America was founded in 1950. It initially operated as the Screen Producers Guild and underwent name changes before adopting its current name. The PGA is open to producers working in film, television, and new media. Membership criteria include having produced a certain number of credits and meeting professional qualifications. Unlike traditional labor unions, the PGA is not a collective bargaining organization. Instead, it focuses on promoting the interests of producers and establishing industry standards. Producers often negotiate individual deals with studios and networks. The PGA is involved in determining producer credits for its members. It has established guidelines to determine which producers receive credit for a particular project, and this process is important for recognizing the contributions of producers to a production.

Like other unions, the PGA presents the annual Producers Guild Awards, which recognize outstanding achievements in film and television production. The PGA Awards are considered significant in the industry and often serve as indicators of success during the awards season. Alongside this, the PGA advocates to address issues relevant to producers and the entertainment industry. It also provides educational programs, workshops, and resources to help producers stay informed about industry trends, technologies, and best practices. The Producers Guild of America awards the "Produced By" credit certification, known as the Producer Mark. This certification is granted to producers who meet specific criteria and have played a substantial role in the production of a film or television project.

Finally, The PGA has various committees that focus on specific areas such as finance, diversity and inclusion, and new media. These committees work on addressing industry challenges, fostering collaboration, and advocating for the interests of producers.

Overall, the Producers Guild of America serves as a professional organization that supports and represents producers in the entertainment industry. While it doesn't function as a traditional labor union with collective bargaining, it plays a crucial role in establishing industry standards, recognizing producer contributions, and providing resources for professional development.

4. **The Writers Guild of America (WGA):** It is a labor union representing writers in the United States working in the fields of film, television, radio, and news media. There are two branches of the WGA: the Writers Guild of America, East (WGAE) and the Writers Guild of America, West (WGAW).

   The WGA was founded in 1933 to address the labor issues and working conditions of writers in the rapidly growing film and radio industries. It has since evolved to include writers in various media formats. Membership in the WGA is open to professional writers who have secured employment under a WGA contract or who are seeking employment as a writer. Joining the union typically requires meeting certain professional qualifications.

   One of the primary functions of the WGA is collective bargaining on behalf of its members. The union negotiates with producers, studios, and networks to establish industry standards for wages, working conditions, residuals, and other terms of employment. The Minimum Basic Agreement (MBA) is the main collective bargaining agreement negotiated by the WGA. It sets the minimum terms and conditions for writers working in the film and television industry. Also, the WGA negotiates residual payment structures for its members. Residuals are additional payments made to writers when their work is rerun, syndicated, distributed on home video, or streamed online.

   Moreover, the WGA plays a crucial role in determining writing credits for its members. The union has specific rules and arbitration procedures to determine which writers receive credit for their contributions to a project. The WGA advocates for the rights and interests of writers, addressing issues such as intellectual property rights, creative control, and fair compensation. Throughout its history, the WGA has engaged in several strikes to assert its members' rights and negotiate better terms. Notable strikes include those in 1960, 1988, and 2007-2008.

In conclusion, the WGA presents its annual awards, the Writers Guild Awards, to honor outstanding achievements in writing for film, television, new media, news, radio, and promotional writing. These awards are significant in the industry and often precede other major awards ceremonies.

Overall, the Writers Guild of America plays a crucial role in protecting the rights and welfare of writers in the entertainment industry. Through collective bargaining, credit determination, and advocacy, the WGA strives to ensure that writers are fairly compensated for their creative contributions.

5. **The International Alliance of Theatrical Stage Employees, Moving Picture Technicians, Artists and Allied Crafts (IATSE)** is a labor union representing a wide range of behind-the-scenes workers in the entertainment industry. IATSE members work in various capacities, including film, television, theater, trade shows, and live events. IATSE was founded in 1893 and has since grown to become one of the largest and most influential entertainment industry labor unions. It represents workers in numerous departments, including cinematography, editing, lighting, sound, makeup, costume design, set construction, rigging, stagecraft, and more. The union covers a diverse range of crafts and trades involved in the production and execution of entertainment projects.

    IATSE membership is open to individuals working in the specified crafts and trades within the entertainment industry. The union provides a collective voice for its members in negotiating terms and conditions of employment. IATSE engages in collective bargaining with employers to negotiate agreements that establish standards for wages, working hours, working conditions, and benefits for its members. These agreements are often specific to different areas of the industry. It places a strong emphasis on safety in the workplace. The union works to ensure that its members have safe working conditions and provides training programs to address safety concerns in various industry sectors. IATSE negotiates contracts that address compensation issues, including residuals for its members. Residuals are additional payments made to workers when their work is reused or distributed beyond its initial airing or release.

Throughout its history, IATSE has engaged in strikes and labor actions to advocate for the rights of its members. These actions are sometimes undertaken to address specific issues, such as unfair working conditions or inadequate compensation.

IATSE is organized into local unions, each representing members in a specific geographic area. These local unions may negotiate their own agreements with employers tailored to the needs of their region.

Furthermore, IATSE provides training and educational programs to its members to enhance their skills, keep them updated on industry advancements, and ensure a highly skilled workforce. IATSE engages in political advocacy to support legislation and policies that benefit its members and the broader entertainment industry.

IATSE's broad representation across various crafts and trades within the entertainment industry makes it a key player in ensuring the well-being and fair treatment of behind-the-scenes workers. The union's activities encompass various issues, from negotiating fair wages to addressing safety concerns and supporting professional development.

POV

Joining a union was not a viable option for me. It's one of those things that you need to decide after you've been working consistently in your niche for a few years for it to be valuable. Unions are not cheap to join, but they provide valuable benefits that protect you in the industry.

My niece decided to join IATSE after she found her way in craft services. She always loved to cook and cater with her dad growing up, and it's something that comes naturally to her. She's worked on popular productions, so joining the union made sense.

Since I was a generalist moving between producing, casting, and coordinating, I hadn't selected a niche. I wanted to learn about all areas and pursue the management and executive track in entertainment. I started working outside the general film and TV industry and secured a full-time stable consulting contract at an organization focusing on entertainment. As I mentioned in earlier chapters, find your niche and what you're good at and then decide if you want to join a union or follow a path similar to mine.

Because of its annual cost, I think most would advise you to gain steady work to ensure you can keep up with your dues rather than risk losing your membership and falling behind. The current IATSE membership is roughly $320 annually and a $1,000 initiation fee.

CHAPTER TEN:

SUSTAIN A SUCCESSFUL CAREER IN THE INDUSTRY

CHALLENGES FACED AS A FREELANCER

Freelancers in the film industry face unique challenges due to the nature of their work. Here are some common challenges:

1. **Irregular Income.** Freelancers often experience fluctuating work opportunities, leading to unpredictable income. Securing consistent projects can be challenging.

2. **Project-Based Work.** Many film industry jobs are project-based, resulting in periods of unemployment between projects. This instability requires freelancers to manage their finances wisely.

3. **Networking and Client Acquisition.** Building a reliable network and consistently acquiring clients or projects is essential. It can be challenging, especially for those starting their careers in the film industry.

4. **Skill Diversification.** Freelancers often need to be versatile, possessing a range of skills beyond their primary role. This adaptability is crucial for securing diverse projects.

5. **Intense Competition.** The film industry is highly competitive, making it challenging for freelancers to stand out. Build-

ing a strong portfolio and maintaining industry connections become vital.

6. **Unpredictable Schedule.** Film projects may have demanding schedules, including long hours and tight deadlines. Balancing work and personal life can be challenging during intense production periods.

7. **Limited Job Security**. Job security is often limited, and freelancers may not have benefits like health insurance or retirement plans provided by employers.

8. **Equipment and Software Costs**. Freelancers are responsible for their equipment and software, which can be expensive. Staying up-to-date with the latest technology is crucial but can strain finances.

9. **Negotiating Rates.** Determining fair and competitive rates for services can be tricky. Freelancers need strong negotiation skills to ensure they are compensated appropriately for their expertise.

10. **Intellectual Property Issues**. Freelancers may face challenges related to the protection of their intellectual property. Understanding contracts and negotiating ownership rights is crucial to avoid disputes.

Navigating these challenges requires a combination of talent, resilience, and business acumen. Building a strong professional network, staying current with industry trends, and continually developing skills can help freelancers thrive in the dynamic film industry.

OVERCOMING FINANCIAL CHALLENGES AS A FREELANCER

Managing cash flow as a freelancer can be challenging, but there are strategies to overcome these hurdles.

Firstly, create a detailed budget to track your income and expenses. Prioritize saving a portion of your earnings for taxes, emergencies, and future goals. Consider using accounting software to streamline financial tracking.

To address irregular income, build an emergency fund to cover essential expenses during lean periods. Diversify your income streams by taking on different projects or clients, reducing dependency on a single source.

Negotiate clear payment terms with clients, such as upfront deposits or milestone payments. Invoice promptly and follow up on overdue payments to maintain a healthy cash flow. Additionally, aim for long-term client relationships to ensure a steady income.

Stay disciplined with your spending habits and avoid unnecessary expenses. Set financial goals, whether short-term or long-term, to guide your budgeting decisions. Consider consulting with a financial advisor for personalized advice on saving and investing to secure your financial future.

Lastly, stay adaptable and continuously reassess your budget and financial strategies as your freelance career evolves.

THE IMPORTANCE OF ADAPTABILITY

Adaptability is a crucial trait, especially for freelancers and professionals in dynamic industries like the film industry. Let's see why it matters.

1. **Navigating Uncertainty.** In rapidly changing environments, adaptability allows individuals to navigate uncertainty and respond effectively to unexpected challenges.
2. **Embracing Change.** Adaptability enables individuals to embrace change rather than resist it. This mindset fosters innovation and a proactive approach to evolving circumstances.
3. **Staying Relevant.** Industries evolve, and skills that are in demand today may not be as relevant tomorrow. Being adaptable allows professionals to stay current and meet evolving market needs.
4. **Diverse Skill Set.** Adaptable individuals are more likely to develop a diverse skill set. This versatility enhances their ability to take on different roles and responsibilities, making them valuable in various contexts.

5. **Resilience in Adversity**. Adaptable individuals demonstrate resilience in the face of adversity. They can bounce back from setbacks, learn from experiences, and use challenges as opportunities for growth.
6. **Effective Problem Solving.** The ability to adapt promotes effective problem-solving. Adaptable individuals are more likely to find creative solutions to complex issues, contributing to their success in various projects.
7. **Thriving in Ambiguity.** Adaptability is especially beneficial in situations of ambiguity. It allows individuals to thrive in environments where the path forward is not clear, making them assets in uncertain circumstances.
8. **Meeting Client Needs**. For freelancers, client needs can vary significantly. Adaptable freelancers can tailor their services to meet diverse client requirements, enhancing their marketability.
9. **Continuous Learning.** An adaptable mindset encourages a commitment to continuous learning. Professionals who embrace new information and skills are better positioned to excel in an ever-evolving landscape.
10. **Building Strong Relationships.** Adaptability fosters effective communication and collaboration. Professionals who can adapt to different communication styles and work preferences build stronger relationships with clients and collaborators.

In essence, adaptability is not just about reacting to change; it's about proactively embracing it. In a world where industries, technologies, and job requirements are constantly evolving, adaptable individuals are better equipped to navigate challenges, seize opportunities, and thrive in their careers.

BUILDING A LOYAL CLIENT BASE THROUGH A REFERRAL SYSTEM

The more your client base grows, the faster you grow in the Film Industry. Therefore, fostering a good and healthy relationship with your clients is necessary. Also, you grow your client base when good referrals are made on your behalf. These are some ways in which you can consistently build a loyal client base:

1. **Deliver Exceptional Quality.** Consistently produce high-quality work. Your reputation for delivering exceptional results is a powerful motivator for clients to refer you to their peers.

2. **Professionalism on Set.** Maintain a high level of professionalism on set. Be reliable, punctual, and collaborative. A positive on-set demeanor contributes to a favorable reputation.

3. **Communication Skills.** Effective communication is key. Clearly understand client expectations, provide regular updates, and be responsive to feedback. Good communication builds trust.

4. **Exceed Expectations.** Go above and beyond what is expected. Surprise your clients with outstanding performance and attention to detail. Exceeding expectations creates memorable experiences.

5. **Build Personal Connections**. Establish personal connections with clients. Show genuine interest in their projects and goals. Building relationships fosters a sense of loyalty.

6. **Consistent Branding**. Maintain a consistent brand image. This includes your online presence, portfolio, and the way you present yourself on set. A cohesive brand strengthens your professional identity.

7. **Offer Incentives for Referrals.** Implement a referral system that rewards clients who refer you to others. This can be in the form of discounts, additional services, or other perks.

8. **Address Issues Promptly.** If challenges arise, address them promptly and professionally. How you handle difficulties can significantly impact how clients perceive your professionalism and reliability.

9. **Seek Feedback**. Actively seek feedback from clients. Use constructive criticism to improve your services. Clients appreciate freelancers who are committed to continuous improvement.

10. **Network Within the Industry**. Attend industry events, build relationships with peers, and collaborate with others in your field. A strong professional network can lead to more referrals.

11. **Showcase Testimonials**. Display positive client testimonials on your website or portfolio. Testimonials serve as social proof of your competence and can influence potential clients.

12. **Be Selective with Projects.** Choose projects that align with your strengths and interests. Successful outcomes are more likely when you are passionate about the work you undertake.

Building a loyal client base is a gradual process that relies on consistently delivering value, fostering positive relationships, and actively managing your professional reputation. Word-of-mouth referrals, driven by your reputation for quality work and professionalism, can become powerful contributors to your freelancing success.

POV

Having longevity in this industry is not easy. It's much easier to work a 9 to 5 job. However, there's a false sense of security that comes with working 9 to 5. Yes, in the beginning, I was flying by the seat of my pants, taking whatever gigs I could get. Still, after a few months, I was on my way—working on projects that lasted anywhere from 3 days to 3 months. It eventually turned into working on only a few projects a year from 25+ projects a year. As the requests for my availability would come in, I was now passing along those referrals to friends.

I made sure my success wasn't dependent on one job. I would never suggest having one source of income in any situation. I started my own media company and explored other avenues to monetize. The industry is cyclical and you have to be prepared for that.

I created and incorporated my business to house my production-related ventures and to give myself a way to still put myself on payroll to pay local and federal taxes toward my social security. You don't want to turn 65 one day and realize you haven't paid anything into social security.

Film and TV is a mostly stable industry that runs 24-hour cycles, but as we have seen in recent events, it too can be subject to shutdowns and layoffs. The entire industry, from acting to writing, went on strike, affecting production work on a major level. Many actors, writers, and technicians went broke for the several months that the strike lasted because they didn't have a rainy day fund. To have longevity in the industry, you need to create multiple revenue streams—like coaching, digital products, etc.

Joining a union is ultimately the wisest choice. However, I didn't find success that way, and I avoided the union altogether. That worked for me, but it may not work for you—especially if you plan to focus on a particular niche covered under IATSE. Still, joining a union requires paying your dues, so you don't want to join prematurely when you don't have enough gigs to warrant paying union fees. Joining a union will guarantee protection if you work consistently on a series after a season or on certain live events yearly.

For me, I was a generalist and went down the management track toward producing. Joining the DGA (directors) or PGA (producers) for directors and producers is a much more stringent process

Everyone's path will look different. There is no one-size-fits-all. It will have a lot to do with your location. More robust film production cities will have multiple TV series, and others will have a more robust event production scene. I suggest incorporating a strategy that allows you to work in TV, film, and event production. That will help you fill in the gaps. The winter seasons are typically the slowest, so having another passive income stream will help you get through those months. I know many people who choose to work seasonal jobs during the off-season when they aren't filming a TV series.

Also, if you aren't good at budgeting or finance, I highly suggest hiring an accountant. You want to be as organized as possible. One of the most miserable things is receiving 15 W2s and multiple 1099 forms to file your taxes. Having a year-round strategy for tax season and a monthly budget that you stick to will save you a lot of time, money, headaches, missed deadlines and, more importantly, eviction. Starting out, it can be feast or famine. So when the money starts flowing in, you may be tempted to splurge on clothes, vacations, fine dining, and massages. This will all come in due time. Just be sure to put some coins away for a rainy day.

CONCLUSION

Finding a niche allows you to focus and deepen your expertise in a specific area of the film industry to become a sought-after professional in your chosen field. A niche sets you apart from the competition. It helps you stand out in a crowded industry and paves the way for you to join a union for added benefits and protections that are necessary if you work long-term in the industry, and it does not require you to obtain a college degree. Or, like me, you can choose to align with a larger organization. However, if you choose to take the management track within an organization and become a generalist, you should pursue higher education to increase your chances of becoming a leader at an organization, studio, or network.

Research and document your leads for production gigs and follow-up. Reach out via email and volunteer for film festivals. If you are lucky, you'll find a good one that pays. On your first gig, always remember to have your business cards and network, network, network. The people you meet may just be the next to hire you. If they do, show up early before your call time. Never stand around and always look busy by volunteering in multiple departments. This will help fast-track you into finding what niche you may fit into. Always hone your skills with online courses. They can fast-track you and provide invaluable advice and knowledge.

If you decide not to choose a niche in technical proficiency or take the executive route and choose to be an independent filmmaker or producer, you must learn about marketing and distribution of your film and pay extra close attention to those film festival gigs. Getting into the film festival itself is a major feat, but nabbing a coveted distribution deal at a festival has been the holy grail of filmmakers. Just recently, Tribeca Films announced its new distribution arm that will offer distribution deals to filmmakers selected during the festival season that will be distributed on SVOD and AVOD platforms like Netflix, Hulu and others. This is a game-changer for indie filmmakers.

You must build a film festival strategy into your marketing plan. Also, ensuring that you have contracts for the rights to the film and that the distribution deal has favorable terms is vital. If you can afford it, you should hire an attorney before you begin to film your project. Hire a seasoned entertainment attorney well-versed in contract negotiation for entertainment deals. Hiring an entertainment attorney is not cheap, but it will save you a major headache down the road.

Hollywood has evolved beyond Los Angeles and is happening all across America. Now is the time to jump in and get your feet wet. You've probably already been editing video content for social media for a few years or managing a production budget to build your content on your social media page. If you are self-taught, you have a headstart in building a portfolio that you can share with department heads with your business card QR code on set as you start to land gigs as a production assistant.

To all those pursuing their passions in the entertainment industry, remember that the journey may have its challenges, but the pursuit of your dreams makes it worthwhile. Embrace the uniqueness of your journey, celebrate your successes, and learn from every experience, whether it's a triumph or a setback. Stay committed to continuous learning and improvement.

The entertainment industry is ever-evolving, and your ability to adapt, innovate, and find joy in the creative process will set you apart. Connect with fellow professionals, seek mentorship, and build a supportive network. As you navigate your path, cherish the moments of inspiration and let them fuel your creativity. Your passion is a driving force that can propel you toward incredible achievements. Trust your abilities, believe in your vision, and keep pushing boundaries. Every project is an opportunity to learn, grow, and contribute with your unique voice. Your dedication to your craft can lead to a fulfilling and impactful career in showbiz. Pursue your passions with vigor, and let your creativity shine.

My industry friends partnering with *Make It in Showbiz* look forward to hearing from you and supporting your journey into the industry. We'll help you identify your most transferable skill set, craft a strategy based on your location, provide feedback on your online portfolio, help improve your skills working with industry pros, and learn how to leverage networking groups to land paid gigs. Scan the QR code below and tell us a little more about yourself.

If you found this helpful and insightful and it motivates you to take the next step forward to launch your career behind the scenes, kindly leave a review post-purchase.

GLOSSARY

1. Equipment

Stinger – An extension cord.

Hot Brick – A walkie-talkie with a fully charged battery.

Legs or Sticks – Simple slang for a tripod.

Clapper – That black-and-white striped board that someone snaps in front of the camera before every take. It displays all the scenes and takes info that the crew needs to sort through the footage at a later date, and the snappy sound it makes is essential for syncing video with the audio during post-production.

Boom Mic – A directional mic mounted to the end of a long pole that is then wielded by sound technician folk to capture close-range audio.

Dead Cat – A fuzzy black cover that goes over the end of a boom mic.

Steadicam – Think Baby Bjorn but for a camera. This stabilizing contraption enables you to strap a camera to your big ol' belly (or rather a vest that you're wearing around your big ol' belly) to get those super smooth shots.

Squib – A tiny explosive device used to simulate a bullet hitting an actor.

Redhead – A type of light with a power rating in the vicinity of 800 watts.

Blonde – Also a type of light but much brighter than a redhead (1,000-2,000 watts).

Dolly – A wheeled cart onto which you mount a camera to capture smooth horizontal shots. Since Steadicams came onto the scene, dollies have slowly been phased out of production. However, there is one shot for which they remain essential, and that is the all-famous Vertigo Effect.

2. People

1st AD – The first assistant director is the second in charge of any set. They serve as the all-important link between the head honcho director and the entire cast and crew and ensure that the production runs like a well-oiled machine.

2nd AD – Working directly under the 1st AD, the second assistant director is responsible for drafting up all the logistical documents (call sheets and the like) and ensuring the 3rd AD has the cast and crew in check.

3rd AD – The third assistant director is one big people wrangler. It's their job to ensure that all cast and crew members are in the right place and at the right time.

Gaffer – Head electrician responsible for setting up all lighting equipment used in a production. You may also hear them being referred to as a Spark or Juicer.

Key Grip – Head technician responsible for setting up all the non-electrical lighting equipment (think lighting modifiers, flags, cookies, etc).

Best Boy – Assistant to either the Gaffer or Key Grip, distinguished by the titles Best Boy Electric or Best Boy Grip.

Second Unit – A completely separate crew charged with filming any takes that don't involve face-to-face interaction, such as inserts and action sequences. Second units usually work alongside the main unit to help speed up the production process.

3. Expressions

Blocking – This is the process of working out where to position all the cameras and lights based on where the actors are going to be standing and moving throughout a scene. This may sound like common sense, but in this case, common sense has a name: blocking!

Rhubarb – Extras pretending to talk to one another in the background of a scene.

Striking – This is what you can expect sound technicians to yell right before they turn one or several lights. It's basically their heads up, it's about to get bright.

10-1 – If you need to use the restroom, don't tell anyone, for this would be poor film set etiquette. Instead, simply yell "10/1" and peace out. Your colleagues will know where you've gone.

Check the Gate – If a director shouts this out, they want the most recent take checked to ensure no impurities (like hair, bugs, arm-waving video bombers) interfered with the lens when recording to film. Today, filmmaking is mostly digital, so it means to play back the media from the card to ensure it was properly recorded.

Flag on the Play – When someone realizes something was wrong with the most recent take and you need to go back to correct it.

Hot Set – A set that is perfectly set up with all of the props, cameras, and lighting in the correct places.

Hold the Red – If someone says this—don't move! Another take is about to happen.

Crowd Base – This is the gathering area where the cast waits before being called onto set (also known as the holding area).

Honey Wagon – Hollywood speak for porta-potties.

Crafty – Short for "craft services," which is short for "catering services."

Video Village – A cluster of viewing monitors where all the directors gather to watch footage being taken.

4. Documents

Call Sheet – This handy little document pretty much spells the Who, What, Where for each day of shooting. Who (as in which actors) will be needed, what scenes are being filmed, and where they're being filmed.

Change Pages – Colored pieces of paper detailing any changes to the script. They're colored differently on purpose so they don't get confused with the existing pages of the script. The more colors you see, the more changes have been made.

Continuity Script – A continuity script is used to record all the itty-bitty details every time a scene is shot—from the length of the actors' hair to what the weather was like to how the set was arranged. This way, if you ever need to go back and reshoot the scene, you can get everything correct.

5. Shots

Extreme Wide Shot – Also known as an establishing shot, extreme wide shots help give the audience some context by showing the building, city, or place where the next scene is about to occur.

Master Shot – Also known as a wide shot, master shots capture all of the relevant actors and actions taking place within a scene. Like extreme wide shots, they're typically used to provide context before jumping to a closer-range shot.

Cowboy Shot – Any shot that shows an actor from the thighs up. These shots were popularized during the Western film era when it was essential for audiences to see the actor's gun holsters.

Mid-Shot – The most popular shot of all. Mid-shots strike the perfect balance between subject and background and typically feature actors from the waist up. Oprah interviews, presenters reading the news, two actors engaged in dialogue—pretty much all of these shots are done at mid-range.

Insert – A close-up of an object filmed separately and inserted into the scene during editing.

OTS Shot – Short for an over-the-shoulder shot. This is where the camera is positioned over one or both of the actors' shoulders in a dialogue scene.

Martini Shot – Last shot of the day. If you hear this, it means your long day on set is coming to an end.

LINGOS ON SET

What is common walkie talkie lingo?

10-1 – "I need to go the bathroom" (number 1).

10-2 – "I need to go the bathroom" (number 2).

10-4 – "I understood the message."

20 – Location; as in, "What's your 20?"

Copy – "I heard and understood the message."

Go Again – "I did not understand the message. Please repeat." You can also say, "Come back on that."

Eyes on… – When someone or something is spotted, as in, "I've got eyes on Spielberg" or "Does anyone have eyes on my lunch box?"

First Team - The principal actors in a scene, as in, "walking the first team to set."

Second Team - The stand-ins for the principal actors.

Lock it Up – "Don't let anyone through." This is usually an instruction to a PA who was told of a door or area they must block.

Flying in – When someone or something is en route, as in, "I'm flying in masking tape."

On it – When you understand the request and are actively working on it. Use only if you have started the work.

Ethan for Nicky – "Ethan" being your name, and "Nicky" being the person you want to reach.

Go for Nicky – The response. "I heard you call for me. What's up?"

Walkie Check – When you first turn on your walkie-talkie. Someone will reply with "Good check," so you know your walkie-talkie's working.

Keying – When someone is accidentally holding down the "talk" button on their walkie, someone will catch it and say "keying" or "someone's keying."

Going off walkie – When you're taking off your walkie-talkie or can't talk anymore.

Spin that, please – When something is said on channel one that needs to be passed along to other channels. This is usually assigned to a key set PA or 2nd 2nd AD before the shoot.

Standby – "I hear you, but I'm too busy to reply."

Standing by – "I've completed the task and am awaiting further instruction."

Strike (or 86) – When something needs to be removed, as in "Strike that prop" or "86 those C-stands from staging."

Kill – When something needs to be turned off, as in "Kill the fog machine."

EXAMPLES OF ADVANCED LINGO

Film set slang is as infinite as it is weird. Now that we're past "What's your twenty," here's some film crew terminology you could hear on a channel:

Martini shot – The last shot of the day. The next shot is "Tequila."

Choker – A tight close-up of eyes only, as in, "Flying in Mr. Depp for the choker."

Baby legs – The legs of a camera tripod.

Bogey – Sometimes "Bogie." It's someone not supposed to be on set.

Four-banger – A large trailer with four doors, a production room, a dressing room, and a crew bathroom.

Hot Brick - A battery with a full charge.

There's more walkie-talkie lingo beyond that, but it gets rather random.

WALKIE TALKIE CODES

Radio etiquette on set matters more than you think it does. Give up your walkie-talkie if someone higher than you runs out of battery. Speak slowly, clearly, and at a moderate volume. Cut back on jokes and other non-sequiturs. Learn your crew's voices to avoid constantly asking who you're speaking with. Be brief and to the point. Bluntness is best.

1. Think before you speak. Concise your point into walkie-talkie codes. Are you saying something offensive? Just think.
2. Wait a beat before you begin to speak. Don't hit the button right when you speak. You'll have to repeat yourself.
3. Be aware of your walkie-talkie's buttons. Don't accidentally switch your dials on or turn down the volume and miss important instructions.
4. Ask twice when needed. While it's always best to say "10-4 over and out," if you don't understand, don't be afraid to ask again. Repeating instructions back can help this.
5. Check your channel often to ensure you didn't forget to switch back.
6. Think about buying your own surveillance earpiece. These are cheap and may be in short supply when you get to the set.
7. Keep your mic a good distance from your mouth while speaking. You don't want your voice to be too loud. 3-5 inches away should be good enough.
8. Make sure your mic wires are underneath the back of your shirt. Loose wires are a danger to yourself and others.

Learning radio etiquette is a matter of experience. However, more often than not, treating a walkie-talkie as a powerful instrument of communication rather than a toy resolves most issues.

Glossary

REFERENCES

The Business of Film: A Practical Introduction, 2018, Second Edition, By Paula Landry & Stephen R. Greenwald.

The Ride of a Life Time; Lessons Learned From 15 Years As The CEO of Walt Disney Company, Copyright @ 2019, By Robert Iger.

Bollywood's $1.3 billion comeback year in 2023 was one of the best of all time by Vineeta Deepak and the Associated Press. Article retrieved from www.fortune.com on December 16th, 2023.

Edison Film and Sound History: The shift to projectors and the Vitascope. Article retrieved from www.wikepedia.com on December 16th, 2023.

Film Careers: The Complete List. Article retrieved from www.careeersinfilm.com on December 14th, 2023

Film Industry in China- statistics and facts. Article retrieved from www.statista.com on January 12th, 2024.

Global box office revenue from 2005-2021(in billion US dollars) published by Statista Research Department.

Article retrieved from www.statista.com on December 15th, 2023.

History of Cinema in the United States. Article retrieved from www.wikepedia.com on December 17th, 2023.

Theatrical Film vs Streaming; Navigating the Post-Covid Entertainment Landscape – A Market Research Perspective by Johnny Anderson. Article retrieved from www.fuelcycle.com on December 14th, 2023.

The 15 Rules of Set Etiquette and What You Should Know About It by Matt Crawford. Article retrieved from www.filmlifestyle.com on December 17th, 2023.

2023 SAG-AFTRA Strike. Article retrieved from www.wikipedia.com on December 17th, 2023.

2023 Writers Guild of America Strike. Article retrieved from www.wikipedia.com on December 15th, 2023.

'A Tribe Called Judah' becomes highest-grossing Nollywood film of 2023 by Anthony Udugba in Business Day online news. Article retrieved from www.businessday.com on January 12th, 2024.

www.ingramcontent.com/pod-product-compliance
Lightning Source LLC
Chambersburg PA
CBHW072057110526
44590CB00018B/3213